Praise for *It's All About At...* YO-BRC-828

"*UNDENIABLY UPLIFTING, FILLED WITH COURAGE, A TRIUMPH!*"

—**Geri Ahearn, CCRN,** Author and Reviewer, Nursing Expertise
for Special Needs Children

Advance praise for *Breathe*

"*I've spent years reading books that promise to help me cure, recover, or remediate. While many have been helpful, few have offered much advice on living with autism, much less on how to do so with grace and joy. This is that book! Here, you will find guidance for living, loving, and thriving now, not in some possible future without autism. Heartfelt, elegant, and accessible, you will go back to this book again and again for hope and inspiration.*"

—**Maria Kowch, BS, CYT,** parent of child with autism,
Yoga Therapist, and Founder, Motion Potions

"*Each day I am presented with the challenge of working with families who are overwhelmed, worn down, and feel greatly unappreciated. They are raw. They are tired. They merely exist. I am captivated by Gayle's guidance to just "breathe." These magical and powerful tools exemplify our ability to not merely exist, but to celebrate, to live, and to love, despite the challenges life may present.*"

—**Diana Davis, M Ed,** Behavioral Consultant

"Breathe *offers ideas all parents can use to improve their lives during the child-rearing journey. Gayle Nobel teaches us how to slow down, notice, reflect and appreciate. In so doing, parents will find moments of insight and peace, even on the hardest days.*"

—**Carrie Sears Bell,** mother of Brian, 19, and Emily, 16

"*We are connected by autism. We are connected by our love for our children. We are connected as mothers looking and hoping to find a friend who understands us, and our children for their abilities, not their disabilities. In* Breathe, *we find the tools to cope, and we learn we are not alone. Thank you, Gayle, for breathing hope and comfort into my soul – for our connection.*"

—**Cathy Logan,** mother of Freddy, 8

"*A delightful, insightful book that focuses on the positives of raising children, and reminds us to take short time-outs to concentrate on ourselves, and* Breathe.*"

—**Robin Schlossman,** Gifted Specialist and CEO, Robin's Resources, LLC

Dr. Norman Vincent Peale once wrote: "Any fact facing us is not as important as our attitude toward it, for that determines our success or failure." As the parent of a child on the spectrum, Gayle Nobel understands the importance of attitude when dealing with the daily challenges of autism. But, she's taken the concept several steps further. This wonderful book is her gift to help us discover and maintain great attitudes to not just survive, but to thrive with autism. Thank you, Gayle!

—**Craig Evans,** Founder, AutismHangout.com

BREATHE

BREATHE

52 Oxygen-Rich Tools for Loving and Living Well with Autism

GAYLE NOBEL

Coauthor of *It's All About Attitude: Loving and Living Well with Autism*

Photography by Rachel Nobel

DESERT
Beach
PUBLICATIONS

Breathe

Copyright © 2010 by Gayle Nobel

For information, contact
Desert Beach Publications
P.O. Box 14
Belleview, FL   34421

www.AutismWithAttitude.com

Editor: Andrea Beaulieu, Andrea Beaulieu Creates, LLC
Cover and Text Design: Bill Greaves, Concept West
Production Editor: Michele DeFilippo, 1106 Design
Photography: Rachel Nobel
Photograph for "Sheer Joy": Neil Nobel
Yoga Pose Photograph for "Falling": Carol Berger Taylor, Metals Edge Studio

Library of Congress Control Number: 2009941550
ISBN-13: 978-0-9777284-1-1

To Leah, Rachel, Kyle, and Neil

Acknowledgements

Thank you to: Carrie Bell, Craig Evans, Cathy Logan, Christy Maxey, Kim Isaac, and Neil Nobel for their eagerness and willingness to take the time to read my first draft and offer valuable insights and feedback.

A special thank you to Carrie Bell who listened tirelessly from the very beginning as I fleshed out my ideas. Her support, wisdom, and encouragement, as both friend and writer, have been a gift.

I am grateful to Sylvia Nobel for planting the first seed for this book long before I was ready to write it; to Robin Asaki for her friendship and listening ear, and for stepping in at the end to help move this process along; and to Sandi Greenberg for always listening and sharing yoga insights, while cheering me on throughout this journey.

Special appreciation goes to Maria Kowch, a fellow traveler on the autism path and one of my prime sources of yoga wisdom. Her yoga classes recharge my body and soul, and inspire my writing. In addition, thanks to the teachers at Yoga Pura, where I have access to an ongoing flow of wonderful inspiration.

With deep appreciation to Kyle's support team: Lolly Laborin, Kim Isaac, Fatima Nasr, Kathleen Walsh, Rich Maston, Roger McLean, and Clint Hacker. By being with Kyle, they have helped me create the breathing space I need in my life to reflect and write. They inspire me with their dedication and attitude.

Thank you so much to Kathleen Walsh and Rich Maston, Kyle's dynamic musical duo. Their music therapy enriches Kyle's life in a big way and was a great source of inspiration for this book.

There is a special place in my heart for Judy Kendall. Not too many people get to have a second mom. She has been there for me in every way along this journey.

An extra, extra special thank you to Kim Isaac for traveling this journey so closely with me. Her wisdom, her special love for Kyle, her unending support for all of us, and her belief in the possibilities, are true gifts.

With appreciation to my creative team:

Andrea Beaulieu worked her editing magic on my stories. Her support, enthusiasm, and creative ideas transformed this book from dream to reality.

Bill Greaves' design talent and enthusiasm made it all work as he blended Rachel's photos with my stories to create something very special.

Michele DeFilippo's technical expertise has been invaluable.

With gratitude to my dear friend and coauthor of *It's All About Attitude*, Kathy Almeida. She noticed the seed for this book had already started blooming before I saw it myself. I appreciate her loving support, inspiration, and friendship, and extend a special thanks to her for believing in my ability to do this on my own.

To my family:

I have great love and deep appreciation for my family. I would like to thank each of them for their ongoing encouragement and support throughout this process.

Leah dazzles and inspires me with her talent and creativity, but more importantly, for being the wonderful person she is. With gratitude for her beautiful song *Attitude is Everything*. She is a special part of my harmony.

Rachel lovingly joined me on this book journey and has been a true delight to work with. I am grateful for the gift of her amazing photography and her beautiful spirit. She handpicked each photo for each story. She is another special part of my harmony.

More than he can ever know, Kyle teaches me how to be a better human being just by being who he is. He is the special soul behind a lot of the wisdom in this book.

I am eternally grateful to Neil, my life partner, my husband, my rock, for taking the high road. He helps me live happily ever after every single day. The best "oxygen-rich tool" I have is our marriage.

CONTENTS

Foreword xiii

Introduction: Welcome To Breathe 1

Appreciation 4

Harmony 7

Gratitude 10

Rest 13

Moments 16

Inspiration 19

Awareness 22

Reach Out 24

Sunrise 27

Thrive 29

Falling 31

Manual Labor 34

Branching Out 37

Differences 40

Breathe Now, and Feel Peaceful 43

Magnificient Moments 46

Tribute 49

The Hard Way 52

The Question 55

Fold Forward 58

Words 61

Music Magic 64

Routines	66
Just Show Up	69
Notice	72
Live Now	75
Gratefulness	78
Next Actions	81
Breathe Now, and Be With What Is	84
Shift	87
Laugh	90
Ask	93
Fast Fix	96
Gratitude in Action	99
Feeling Good	102
Balance	104
Resilience	107
Pages	109
Silence	112
Quotes	114
Nothing	117
It Is What It Is	120
Exercise	123
Breathe Now, for Nourishment	125
Heart's Desire	128
Just One Thing	131
Mentor	134
Jewels	136
Scary	138
Sheer Joy	141
Wishes	144
Zen	147
Epilogue: Ready to Launch	150

Foreword

Gayle is my friend. She is also a wife, a mother, and an amazing human being. She has been an advocate for those she loves who have autism since first encountering it with her brother, and then with her son. Now she extends that support to others.

As a seasoned traveler on this path, in *Breathe* she offers easy, doable, and approachable tools, providing insight and nourishment for the journey ahead. While this book is about her journey with autism, the tools she shares will work for any one of the many challenges we face in life. Make no mistake about it – it takes courage to love and live well. Each of us can use a little help along the way.

Long ago, when Gayle and I first became friends, we often joked about the fact that no handbook existed to help us along our way. We had no idea where we were going or what to do. It was new to us – this autism country. Today, she is doing just that – offering a handbook intended to encourage, support, and love you in the special assignment you have been given.

The other night I watched a fictional medical drama about a man who had an inoperable tumor. No one would operate on him. He asked the top surgeon in the field to do it. The surgeon replied, "No, because what you have is impossible to cut. What you have is inoperable. If I were to try, you would mostly likely die, or at the very least, end up paralyzed."

The patient proceeded to share how he had lost his family, first his parents, then his beloved wife and children. Finally, he had lost his homeland to war. He had survived each of those losses and was willing to take the risk of surgery, even if it meant he would lose the use of his legs, or quite possibly his life.

The surgeon said, "But there's no way."

The man continued his plea declaring that when everything looks impossible, that's the time to get inspired. That's the time to create a new way. The surgeon chose to perform the surgery and was successful in not only removing the tumor, but also in saving the patient's life and the use of his legs.

Even though this was a fictional story created for primetime, it could be true. Believe there is a new way, and that you, too, can create it.

I love and admire my friend, Gayle, for all she is and has done. She is a very special human being. As you read this book, know that now is your time to get inspired. Gayle is your guide, helping you through the troublesome spots. She is your friendly navigator helping you create a new way.

—Kathy Almeida, coauthor, *It's All About Attitude*

WELCOME
TO *BREATHE!*

If you are the parent of a child with autism, perhaps you have searched long and hard for that one thing, the quick fix, the magic answer, only to discover it does not exist. Or, maybe you are just beginning this journey and are feeling scared, lost, or overwhelmed. You may feel as if you barely have a moment to catch your breath in the whirlwind of life that is autism. Weary or depleted, you might be in need of some well-deserved nourishment. In the form of stories and oxygen-rich tools born of my own journey with autism, *Breathe* is that source of nourishment.

Through *Breathe*, I am whispering directly into your ear, because I have a heart and soul connection with you. We are walking on parallel paths, taking journeys that ask very special and unique things of us. We are challenged daily by loving and living with children who are not easy. Our lives are packed with obstacles sometimes too large to surmount. In many ways, the obstacles on our path ARE the path.

At the same time, these stories and tools are equally valuable to those who do not have a loved one with autism. Autism becomes a metaphor for the unexpected life challenges we all face, in one form or another.

Why *Breathe*? Last year, I watched my son, Kyle, who is deeply affected by autism, calm himself in the emergency room with his breath. Instinctively, he seemed to know what to do. I realized, perhaps I need look only as far as my son for one of life's magic answers. (See "Zen" for the full story.)

Breathing is, indeed, very powerful, when we use it fully. Unfortunately, when we are stressed, agitated, or overwhelmed, our breath tends to be short and shallow. We use only a tiny fraction of our lung capacity to nourish ourselves with life's fuel – oxygen.

Breathing deeply is my prescription for creating enhanced feelings of well being. I've found it helps me regroup and calm down. Breathing often serves as an automatic attitude adjuster. I stop for a moment and take five deep breaths. By breath number five, a shift – albeit tiny – has usually taken place. Then, rather than react to Kyle, I often am better able to guide him. We both benefit.

Life with autism asks some hard questions. I share my stories so I can hold your hand as we explore those questions together. Through my personal experiences, I am delighted to present some powerful, life-tested tools. These are my special elixirs that continue to help me thrive, rather than merely survive my lifelong journey with my son, Kyle. These tools fill my *It's All About Attitude* toolbox. They refill my personal well. They help make loving and living well with autism real.

There are no quick fixes for your child in *Breathe*. These stories and oxygen-rich tools do have the power to help you see your child and your life through a different lens. Ultimately, they may help you heal. As you heal, your child benefits, because you are better equipped to support and nurture him or her, as well as your entire family.

Just as the breath oxygenates our cells, these oxygen-rich tools have the power to create a ripple effect in your life, transforming your attitude and your journey, one micro-movement at a time. If you stand back, you are likely to notice a tiny shift in your personal landscape.

So, I invite you to indulge yourself. You are definitely worth it. I have heard from so many there just isn't the time. I'm with you, and I hear you! That's why each oxygen-rich tool takes five minutes or less. I have provided one tool for each week of the year, or to play with whenever the spirit moves you. Move at your own pace, but start.

How you live your days is how you live your life. It all starts with breathing. How long has it been since you've taken a long, deep breath?

Love, live well, and enjoy!

Oxygen-Rich Tool

On your mark, get set, BREATHE. Stop "doing" for a moment. Take five deep breaths. Focus on breathing more slowly and deeply. Repeat as often as needed. Refills for this prescription are unlimited, and ideally, habit-forming.

APPRECIATION

Who was lying on the floor of the hospital intensive care room with me when Kyle, our six-month-old baby, was seizing uncontrollably?

Who held me as I cried, the night we realized Kyle was most likely autistic?

Who tried so hard to make eye contact with his son he shined a flashlight on his own face while under a sheet, in hopes of creating a tiny connection?

Who dove right in with me as we waded through therapies for Kyle, often to find they did not provide the answers we were seeking?

And who recently got up to care for Kyle when we were both very sick? Who looked at me and said, "I'll do it"? "I owe you one," I groaned. "Nope," he said, "we're a team. This is what I do for my partner."

Who? My rock, my teammate, my lifeline of support – my husband, Neil – who still stands beside me after all these years as we celebrate the baby steps we call progress.

Thank you. Thank you. Thank you.

Though *Breathe* is my journey, and Neil would probably have a different story to tell, we always have stood together as a team, supporting each other and working together for the greater good of our family.

Fortunately, we never lost sight of what brought us together in the first place. Our special partnership – our marriage – remains strong. Husbands often stand in line behind children, too easily taken for granted and pushed to the sidelines. This is magnified when there is a child with special needs in the family. It's easy to become complacent. In fact, it's so easy I got to the end of this book and discovered a gaping hole in my story. I had not acknowledged the debt of gratitude I owe Neil.

Expressing appreciation is a powerful stepping stone on this path. It is one that can never be revisited too often. Neil didn't sign up to walk this path. Unlike me, he had no preparation or education.

Autism has the power to make even the strongest person feel incompetent as a parent. Rather than crumbling, Neil has risen to the occasion time and again, standing strong and tall in his role as father to Kyle and our daughters. Hand in hand, we have walked this journey together, learning to love and live well in uncharted waters, reinventing ourselves both individually and together as we went along. Neil has become more than I ever could have envisioned.

I believe a heartfelt expression of gratitude is a power booster for loving and living well on our life's journey. So to my husband, Neil, I say thank you. Thank you for taking the high road, the rockier road, when you could have abandoned the ship a long time ago. But, that is not who you are, and I knew that from the very start. In good times and in tough times, for better or for worse, you have been my teammate and my rock. I have never felt alone.

Oxygen-Rich Tool

Who holds your hand? Who is your rock? Look that person in the eye and express your heartfelt appreciation. The more detail, the better. Is there a lump in your throat? Say it anyway. Ultimately, it feels so good.

HARMONY

I have three children: my son, Kyle, who has autism, and my two daughters, Rachel and Leah, who don't. My daughters were born after Kyle.

I could easily have been swallowed up completely by the world of autism without the arrival of my daughters. Kyle had already experienced many extreme medical and developmental issues by the time the girls came along.

They provided a sort of equilibrium to our lives. Kyle was perched on one side of the motherhood scale, and my girls sat together on the other. However, the scale was never really balanced, at least not by reaching some elusive state where everything felt level and stable. In terms of time and energy, Kyle's needs had to take precedence over those of my daughters.

There's an aha moment here. Balance is a myth. This journey is really about harmony. The reality is that having Kyle offered me perspective – that very often, things work together for good. There is harmony, even if it doesn't look like it initially.

My daughters seemed to grow and develop like flowers. With nurturing, attention, and opportunities, they blossomed easily. It felt like magic compared to Kyle's delayed and spotty development. Yet, without my experience with Kyle, it would have been natural to cruise through my daughters' childhoods on autopilot. Instead, his challenges actually ignited within me a deep appreciation for the relative ease of raising my girls. I took little for granted. I never missed a dance recital, school performance, graduation or bedtime story. It may have been a rough day with Kyle, but at the end of the day, I was there for my girls.

While the scale was never balanced, there was harmony in my family, and in my life. In the grand scheme of things, everyone received the support they needed, and my girls learned to be patient, self-sufficient, and independent.

Oxygen-Rich Tool

How is harmony operating in your life, and in your family? Sometimes it takes some looking, but it is there. Set aside five minutes, grab a piece of paper and a pen, and start writing. Begin with whatever comes to mind. Want to take it up a notch? Buy a journal and some great pens. Notice what wonderful things you learn.

GRATITUDE

"It is my love for Kyle that carries me through the difficult moments in life. When I can focus on that true love, I find a deeper peace and happiness. In the final hour, 'love wins,' and it is Kyle who has shown up to deliver that message over, and over, and over again." (It's All About Attitude, 2006)

Yes, love *does* win. But, some days I feel discouraged and out of touch with that love. Some days are just plain tough. That's when I focus on gratitude.

I used to think gratitude was a magical feeling that somehow would come over me when something really great happened. I've since grown to see gratitude as an attitude – a stance toward life. Gratitude is a mental and emotional muscle that gets stronger the more I use it. With gratitude, I do more than survive this journey with autism. With gratitude, I thrive.

Gratitude is a decision I can make moment by moment. Sometimes, I am able to make that decision. Other times, because the moments are so fast and intense, I live in reaction mode. I might easily slip into a default position of negativity and discouragement. Maybe I don't have as much patience as I normally have. Maybe I feel fatigued. Maybe Kyle is demanding more than I can provide, or doing things I find irritating. Or, perhaps some incident just pushes me over the edge and I wish I didn't have to deal with this "autism thing."

At the end of the day, if it's been one of those days, making the decision to feel grateful makes gratitude real. I make a list of the things I love about Kyle. I allow my hand to glide across the page as fast as it can. Even a list of just five things makes gratitude tangible and creates a tiny shift in my attitude. I'm always glad I did this because, once again, love wins, and it feels really good.

Oxygen-Rich Tool

This will take less than five minutes. Take pen to paper and list all the things you love about your child. Write as quickly as possible until you reach the bottom of the page. If you get stuck, repeat something. Then, write more if the spirit moves you.

REST

Living with autism is like climbing a very tall, steep mountain. It's often rocky or slippery. I make mistakes and I get scared. I might stumble or slip. Sometimes, I even fall. There are twists, and turns, and surprises along the journey. There are usually challenges, too. Sometimes, I come to a fork in the road and I have no idea which way to go. Other times, I might even have to backtrack or turn around for a while. I have to take the trail as it comes.

When climbing a mountain, it's important to pace myself, stopping along the way to recharge. I find the same to be true of living with autism. If I try to race to the top, there's a chance I might not make it. I will wear out or burn out on the trail. Though my agenda or my ego might try to convince me I don't need to rest, I try to listen closely to my body and spirit. They don't function very well on empty. To stay on the path, I need to rest and refuel.

Over the years, I've found if I can bring the same wisdom to living with autism – to pause and rest at least once during the day, even for just a short amount of time – life feels better, and so do I. When I slow down my pace, I also miss a lot less along the way.

My favorite resting pose is one of the basics of yoga – child's pose. Child's pose requires no equipment and is excellent for resting and recharging. Frequently, I don't have time to indulge in child's pose, so I do it anyway. Not having time is one of the signs of "dehydration" along the journey with autism, or for that matter, the journey of life.

Like a baby taking a nap, I curl face down on the carpet into the smallest ball I can form. My mind wants to talk to me, and it does. I try not to get caught up in the conversation. The longer I stay, the better I feel. My back smiles, my soul smiles, and for a time, I am at peace.

Oxygen-Rich Tool

Try child's pose. This is best done on carpet, folded blankets, or a yoga mat. Start on your hands and knees, and then push yourself back until your bottom is resting on your heels. Let your torso and head drop to rest on the floor. Place your arms back along your sides. Stay in this position, breathing and relaxing for as long as you can.

MOMENTS

I got a phone call from my husband, Neil. It went something like this:

"Have you started dinner yet?"

"Just starting it."

"I would like to take you and Kyle out to dinner to celebrate the end of the month."

Though dinner was partially started, I jumped at the opportunity.

It was late. It was at least an hour and a half past Kyle's usual dinnertime. The restaurant we chose – one that Kyle enjoys and is familiar with – turned out to have a very long wait, so we decided to go somewhere else. This is not so easy for someone with autism. Kyle got excited just walking across the parking lot, but we had to switch gears and turn around. He went with the flow.

Thinking fast, we remembered the new gluten-free pizza restaurant across the street. It, too, was crowded, and there were no booths available to provide the structure so helpful to Kyle. Instead, we were seated at an awkward metal table outside with the traffic noise, lots of lights in the background, and a crying baby, where we waited for our food. Kyle handled the uncertainty and obstacles with grace. He remained quiet and relatively calm. We stayed calm too, and even ventured into the realm of typical dinner conversation.

We were having a moment.

Satiated with gluten-free pizza, it was time to leave. The patio was now packed, and I knew how much Kyle wanted to run. He rose to the challenge of getting up slowly. I followed along as Dad confidently guided him through the narrow maze of people and food-filled tables. Kyle calmly followed. My two guys were at their best.

From beginning to end, this was an evening of moments.

For many families, having an easy dinner on Friday night is probably typical and taken for granted. For us, it was anything but typical, and we certainly didn't take it for granted. This was the first time it didn't feel "hard" to be with Kyle in a restaurant. Dining out as a threesome was actually enjoyable and comfortable.

I thought about what brought us to this place in time. There were so many roadblocks and unexpected twists and turns. How did we get here? There was no magic formula; just persistence, I suppose. Believing in more than what we could see. Trusting ourselves, yet also allowing others to teach and help. Growing in our own roles as guides in the school of relationships and life, as Kyle grew as apprentice.

And, watching for those moments.

Oxygen-Rich Tool

Watch for your moments. They will come. Moments pack an extra punch when you share them with someone, so pick up the phone.

INSPIRATION

Do one thing every day that inspires you. I've decided these are words to live by.

I'm certain that inspiration increases endorphins, but without the calories of chocolate. Inspiration keeps me from drying up, particularly on those days when I'm feeling discouraged or worn down. Inspiration is the tiny ray of sunshine that enters my heart in small, yet powerful, doses.

Inspiration by way of my daughters and their art packs an extra zing.

Just looking at a photograph taken by Rachel brings me joy and peace. In one particular photo, the sun is setting over the beach in the north of France. The ocean is glistening. The colors are magnificent. Of course, it's not just the picture. It goes well beyond that. I am reminded of Rachel's zest for travel and how she goes after life experiences with gusto and passion. Her photography inspires me, and so does the person behind the camera.

I get inspired just listening to a song written by Leah – *I Will Hold You In My Heart*. It plays over and over in my mind. Normally, I would find this irritating, but there are so many things I love about this song. I am moved by how wise and insightful her lyrics are, especially when I compare them to the shallow lyrics I often hear. And, because she makes art out of ordinary life, and it works. When I listen, I smile on the inside and on the outside. It's not just the song, but the passion of the artist, who happens to be my daughter.

I am moved by the art of my daughters. Their music and photography are a reflection of their passion and creativity. It's part of who they are. It is another way to get to know them – a window into their soul – and I am inspired.

Inspiration is another brand of love. However it appears – through music, art, quotes, people, events, places – it is always there. I have only to decide to take it in.

Oxygen-Rich Tool

Savor a little piece of inspiration. It will help fill you up. Do one thing, something, anything that inspires you.

AWARENESS

If you do what you always do, then you're gonna get what you always got.

It's easy to live on autopilot. I find myself repeating the same behaviors or reactions, even if they aren't working. Then I wonder why Kyle's responses or actions don't change either. We both get stuck.

What's the solution? Cultivating awareness.

When I tweak a response or reaction – something I usually do or say – it freshens life up a bit. First, I have to notice the patterns. Then, I can decide to make a different choice. The side effect is Kyle often makes a shift or takes a step forward on his path of growth. It tends to have the same effect on me.

For example, Kyle sits at the same spot at the kitchen table every day. He often leaves the table so rapidly I can't guide him to take his dish to the sink and wash his hands. I, in turn, go into high speed and try to bring him back into the kitchen so he can take care of these things. This doesn't work, and nothing changes.

The other day, I changed his seat at the table. Kyle wasn't able to operate on autopilot and neither was I. It made a difference. He got up much more slowly and accepted my guidance with his dishes and his hands. Both of us experienced much less resistance and struggle.

When I choose to live consciously, rather than unconsciously or out of habit, I'm always glad I did. It makes life more interesting, more fun, and much richer.

Oxygen-Rich Tool

Tweak something. Make an adjustment. Change a pattern. It might be something you always do or say. Possibly, it's a reaction or a habit. Decide, just once, to do it differently. Make it a small thing, and be creative.

REACH OUT

Kyle's autism and other developmental issues have brought our family a tremendous set of challenges. While the journey has been rewarding and filled with growth, it has not been an easy one. In fact, there have been several, very distinct, dark periods when it was pretty tough to feel a glimmer of happiness, or conjure up anything resembling gratitude. Knee deep in the muck, all I could see was muck. My focus was on survival – getting through the day, or maybe the hour, or perhaps even just the minute.

Kyle had severe and frequent seizures in early childhood. Then, beginning in puberty and lasting into early adulthood, he experienced debilitating anxiety. These were very trying times during which I felt emotionally drained. Kyle's life held few moments of quality. He seemed to be suffering, and it's hard to watch your child suffer. Though I have always subscribed to the idea that loving and living well with autism was all about my attitude, there were times when I could not create a flicker of an attitude that would lead me to living well. I could not find a shred of gratitude, or anything resembling a sense of humor. These were definitely not on my radar.

When I was struggling in crisis mode, I couldn't detect any light at the end of the tunnel. Feeling good, focusing on the positive, and seeing things differently felt far out of my reach. It was hard to be my best for Kyle. I had to find a way to take care of myself. What could I do?

Reach out. Reach out for support. What helped move me through the darkness and out into the light was my support system. If it hadn't been for my husband and other children, and my friend and coauthor, Kathy Almeida, I might have allowed life to swallow me up completely.

Kathy also has a son with autism. The way Kathy and I have been there for each other, supporting and embracing each other from afar, was, and still is, one of the keys for each of us to cultivate an attitude that helps us love and live well with autism. Not that the times were always good, or that we didn't sometimes struggle to appreciate our sons or the lessons we were learning along the way. Only that, when we were in the depths of *whatever*, we knew the other was just a phone call or an email away. When one of us couldn't see the good, learn the lesson, or change our attitude, we could turn to the other. It didn't matter how we showed up on those phone calls, the other was there with an open heart, open ears, and open arms.

Oxygen-Rich Tool

Make the phone call. Write the email. Reach out for support. You don't have to be in crisis mode to benefit. A five-minute conversation with a supportive friend or family member is powerful stuff. Just writing an email to someone who understands and cares can create a shift even before you receive the reply.

SUNRISE

After a hectic morning, the invisible hand of my wiser self pushed me out the door. My to-do list would still be here when I returned, and I knew a short hike would do me a world of good. Without pausing to clean up the morning mess, I stepped out into a beautiful, overcast, balmy morning. Phoenix is not usually gray, and definitely not balmy, but occasionally we get some moisture and it's a real treat.

My mind was busy most of the way up the mountain, so I didn't really notice the surrounding desert beauty until I got to the top. It only takes about twenty-five minutes to reach the summit of the small mountain behind my house, but I never fail to shift into a different mental and emotional state by the time I arrive.

Today, I was greeted by the tail end of an amazing sunrise. The glimmer of a pink-orange sun behind the silhouette of purple-blue mountains in the distance took me by surprise. My thoughts and concerns suddenly felt insignificant in the larger scheme of things. My mood lifted instantly.

It had been a very long time since I'd seen a sunrise. Perhaps I'm just feeling more sentimental as I approach my birthday, but I decided it would be magnificent to have this experience more often. The sun comes up later in Arizona in the winter because we don't change our clocks. Maybe there's an opportunity lurking here. If I can soak up a sunrise once in a while, it might help set the tone for the rest of my day. And possibly, as I did today, I'll see a pack of coyotes doing the same.

Oxygen-Rich Tool

Treat yourself to a sunrise this week. Cost: free. Time investment: a few moments. Possible side effect: a tiny shift in your awareness or mood.

Pack of coyotes: bonus.

FALLING

"**Falling.** It's the one time we get to practice getting up." My yoga instructor shared this piece of wisdom with me, and I love it. She was talking about falling out of a pose. In yoga, we often practice poses that require balance, stability, and concentration. On a deeper level, they also call for compassion and acceptance.

These poses are challenging. Some days I am steadier than others. At times, I spend more time falling out of a pose than standing in it. Falling becomes an opportunity to learn something about myself. It's all good. At least, I would like to think it is. I'm working on that.

It took me many years of practice to begin to experience what yoga is really about. I am just beginning to taste the deeper meanings and bring them into my life. Yoga goes beyond stretching and moving. It is really a laboratory of life lessons practiced in a controlled environment; in this case, on the yoga mat. All the issues that come up during practice are the same ones that surface in my life – self-criticism, comparing myself to others, impatience, and perfectionism. Just one pose can conjure up this entire list, plus more.

My goal is to notice my response to falling, pick myself up graciously, and maybe even smile. Hmm, sounds a lot like life, doesn't it?

Oxygen-Rich Tool

I challenge you to play with tree pose today. If you fall, smile and start over. **Warning:** *standing in tree pose on a regular basis may improve your balance.*

Here's how to get there:

1. Stand with your feet together.

2. *Put your weight on your left foot, feeling the ground with your left foot as you prepare to balance.*

3. *Pick up your right foot and find your balance. Bend your right leg, placing the sole of your right foot on the inside of your left thigh, calf, or ankle.*

4. *Press your right foot into your left thigh, calf, or ankle.*

5. *Once you have your balance, bring your hands together at your heart and breathe.*

Repeat on the other side.

MANUAL LABOR

Leah and I packed the car with painting supplies and drove two hours to her new apartment in Flagstaff, Arizona. Our mission: to paint her room.

We had already visited Home Depot, where there was considerable fumbling looking for the correct tools and supplies. I had not even thought about painting a room since before Kyle was born, so this was unfamiliar territory.

We reached our destination. Now came the hardest part of the job, and the part I would much prefer to skip – preparation. With painting, it's all about the preparation. It seemed to take forever before we actually got the rollers wet and began to paint. But, finally, milk chocolate paint was gliding onto the textured walls, and I was learning how to paint again.

I had forgotten how physically demanding it was. Bending, reaching, pushing – working out at the gym might have been easier. However, there is something about manual labor. Zap! It pushes me right into the present moment. Nothing is more important than getting the brown paint into all those corners without smearing it on the white ceiling. Oops, easier said than done. Painter, I am not. Though, for that day, I was.

What does this have to do with living with autism? Nothing. That's the point. Thank goodness for manual labor.

I was surprised at how good I felt doing it. All the issues that had been floating around in my head melted into the milk chocolate paint. They just didn't exist while I was prepping, and painting, and joking with Leah. It felt really good to be there for my daughter, helping her create a pretty nest. As my girls get older, days like this are few and far between.

That evening, I glided home in gratitude. It was a long, two-hour drive, but we had accomplished a lot. I was exhausted, but in a very

35

satisfied, paint-splattered way. Touch ups were left for another trip. We had something nice to show for all our hard work.

Oxygen-Rich Tool

Do something with your hands – something that requires physical effort. Clean. Organize. Five-minute projects abound. But, watch out. You might look up and notice thirty minutes have gone by, and you have been totally engrossed in your job. It's all about the process – all physical, no heavy thinking required.

BRANCHING OUT

I confess. I am addicted to the to-do list. By making lists, I stay focused and don't forget important things. I've also brainstormed my way through many decisions by making lists. However, a few months ago, I felt stuck. Kyle had been attending his day program for more than two years, and I was still very dissatisfied with it. When an opportunity to make a change presented itself, I felt uncertain and afraid to move forward. I kept coming back to questions I had asked many times before. What's best for Kyle? What is my vision for his life?

I had recently read about the mind mapping process in a health book. The book explained that mind mapping is a great tool when you are feeling overwhelmed by a task. It flexes parts of the mind you might not use as often, like those associated with imagination. I was curious and decided it was worth a try.

Rather than listing items in a linear fashion, you draw your subject in the center, then draw branches out from the center, like spokes on a wheel, leading to your ideas. I drew a great looking stick figure with curly hair (Kyle) in the center of a piece of paper. I then drew branches from Kyle to keywords that summarized important areas of his life. From each area, I branched out to subcategories, getting more and more detailed. My mind began moving faster than my pen. Almost effortlessly, new ideas and thoughts started appearing on the page. I began to feel excited and motivated to move forward in a new direction. I had discovered the possibilities of the mind map.

Apparently, mind mapping exercises the brain in a different way than the linear list. According to the book, *YOU, Staying Young,* by starting in the center, you give your brain the freedom to spread out in different directions. This helped me get past that feeling of being stuck.

Our brains work by association. By connecting the branches, we understand, remember, and act on an issue much more easily. I was taking a new route to address a difficult decision. At the same time,

I also was exercising my mind by creating new pathways. These new pathways lead to a new pathway for Kyle.

I'm still addicted to my lists. But now, when I'm feeling especially stuck or overwhelmed, or I need to inject some creativity into a situation, I turn to the mind map. It makes problem solving a little easier, and definitely more fun.

Oxygen-Rich Tool

Looking for some creative ideas? Need to address an issue? Try the mind map. Your mind will love the freedom. You may even surprise yourself with a few, new, bright ideas.

DIFFERENCES

W had guests at our cabin this past weekend. Our friend and his two little girls were in the area and decided to pay us a visit one evening. Decked out in matching pink and white Nikes, and exhibiting some amazingly curly hair, Nadya and Elanah were the image of our own daughters when we first built our getaway. At ages three and five, their beautiful childlike energy and curiosity quickly filled our cabin.

Kyle, in his usual style, retreated back to his comfort zone – his bedroom. The rest of us were visiting, talking, and playing. It wasn't too long before we decided it was time to dive into the dessert our guests had brought. As I was scooping out the mint chocolate chip ice cream, Kyle suddenly appeared. Kyle doesn't usually join in when company is in the house, particularly if there is a lot of commotion. Plus, ice cream is not normally a food he goes for. But, there he was, right in the middle of the social action. Dairy free diet aside, I felt compelled to welcome him by offering him some ice cream.

The girls had never met anyone like Kyle, and the questions began to flow. In her beautiful innocence, five-year-old Elanah had no notions of correctness. Without judgment or fear, she asked what was in her heart, and on her mind:

"Why doesn't he talk?"

"Why does he make those sounds?"

"Can he take care of himself?"

"Will he ever be able to move to an apartment?" (Yes, a five-year-old asked this – don't you love it?)

It's so good for little ones to be with people who are different. With that in mind, I welcomed the questions.

One question quickly led to another. Eventually, she wanted to know who would take care of Kyle when I wasn't here anymore. By the look on her face, she was clearly worried. I reassured her there would always be someone to look after Kyle. I was in awe of how quickly she got to a question that often weighs heavily on my mind, too.

Soon, we were on to lighter questions, and the ice cream. Kyle also was eating pretzels, and they were falling into his ice cream. "Why is he doing that?" Elanah wanted to know. (I love being with young children when it comes to Kyle. Their pure innocent curiosity bubbles forth like water from a spring.) Making light of it, I told her pretzels and ice cream might taste good together. In an instant, she had sprinkled her ice cream with Kyle's gluten-free pretzels. She discovered she liked the concoction! While Kyle only had one or two pretzels submerged in his melted ice cream, she loaded hers to the top. She savored every bite. Her pleasure was delightful.

On the other hand, my quiet joy in watching her join Kyle was also bittersweet. I saw in her response – acceptance of Kyle, just as he is – the change I would like to see in the world. I know that change starts with me, and I know that making light of our "differences" is one way to create that change.

It's all about attitude. What I say or do, and how I say or do it, are what matter to the world as it watches. People gain their vision, perception, beliefs, and eventually, comfort level, in part by what they observe from the people close to Kyle, and others like him. That night, making light of his differences made a difference for two sweet little girls. It made a difference for me, too. And for Kyle, it *was* the difference.

Oxygen-Rich Tool

Be the change you wish to see in the world. Find an opportunity to make light of something. You may even notice those around you doing the same.

If all else fails, try some pretzels in your ice cream.

BREATHE NOW, AND FEEL PEACEFUL

$Stop,$ just for this moment, and take a deep breath. Breathe deeply, filling your belly as well as your lungs. Count as you breathe in. Count as you breathe out. Breathe in and out for the same number of counts. Do this for as long as you can. Even just a minute can make a difference.

How do you feel? Calmer? More peaceful? This is what the breath can do. Transport us into that feeling of stillness and present-moment awareness. Just the place we want to be when we are with our loved ones.

I became acquainted with the power of the breath through my yoga practice. Yoga is one of my passions. At first, it was only about the physical aspects – the stretching and exercises, with a little relaxation thrown in at the end. Over the years, I have slowly discovered so much more. I find myself looking forward to the theme of each class as much as I do the movements and poses. Now, given the profound feeling of well being I experience after class, I can't imagine life without yoga.

The other day, my favorite teacher, Maria, was discussing the yoga toolbox. She asked what we found most helpful. What do we turn to when we are feeling stressed? Inevitably, most of us came back to the foundation of yoga, the breath.

She pointed out something I had never considered. Respiration is the only system that is both autonomic AND in our control. In that way, it can be a linked to other autonomic systems in the body affected by stress, such as digestion, heart rate, and cognition.

Back in the days when we were fighting the wooly mammoth, our bodies were designed for fight or flight. In the midst of one of these, our bodies were pumped with adrenaline. Our elevated heart rate gave us the zip we needed to take care of ourselves. Though the wooly mammoth is long gone, our physical response to stress is often still the same.

At one time, autism was my wooly mammoth. And, it was much more about fight than flight. In my encounters with many parents of those with autism, they experience the same thing. After a while, it can take a toll on both one's physical and mental well being.

When I'm feeling worried or anxious, my breathing is often shallow. In fact, I am not even aware of breathing. I might be holding my breath or breathing rapidly. Though I might not be able to change my thoughts or circumstances in that moment, I can remember to breathe. When I focus on my breath, my mind can't help but become quiet. Brain fog begins to lift, and the doorway to clearer thinking starts to slide open.

Unlike most things in life, we can control the quality of our breath. The breath is free, always available, and very powerful. The breath. Ahhhh.

Oxygen-Rich Tool

The breath is one of the simplest, yet most powerful, tools you own. Take five. Allow yourself a breath break. Breathe consciously. Breathe deeply. Breathe into your belly. Breathe with awareness. Put your own oxygen mask on first. Then you can be there for others.

MAGNIFICENT
MOMENTS

Kyle

Kyle was in music therapy today. I watched from the observation room as three people created a melody together, each making their own passionate contribution to the music. They were in sync and in rhythm. For the music therapists, the motions came easily. For my son, Kyle, the coordination of his two hands, voice, and eyes was nothing short of spectacular. For me, it was as if time stood still.

I never know what a session will bring for Kyle. Today, it brought one of those magnificent moments.

Kyle was playing a drum in time to Kathleen's voice and guitar. Rich played too, as he and Kyle balanced the drum across their laps. At times, Kyle is simply unable or unwilling to hold anything in his hands. Some days he is silent and others, loud. Some days it is harder for him to sit still and focus. He is consistently inconsistent. Today, Kyle was a full participant, using both his hands, plus his voice, to make glorious music with his therapists, his friends. He played with zest and determination.

Just when I couldn't imagine it getting any better, Kyle looked across the drum to Rich. Face to face, eye-to-eye, he made a connection. He maintained this for the rest of the song, briefly looking away and then back again. Eye contact does not come easily for Kyle, particularly when his other senses are engaged. This was miraculous.

What could be better? I found out after the session was over, that Kyle shifted his gaze in response to Rich changing the beat. Kyle responded to an unexpected change with his eyes, just as I might have done, and then quickly made an adjustment in his own rhythm. Amazing.

I thought about this on the long drive home. I shared the experience with Neil. Then, I wrote it down so I could read it and revel in it during leaner, less magnificent days to come.

Oxygen-Rich Tool

Be on the alert for a magnificent moment. Find one tiny experience with your child to celebrate. Record this in a gratitude journal, or start a special "magnificent moments" notebook. Then, at the end of those days that feel as if they will never end, treat yourself to a taste of magnificence.

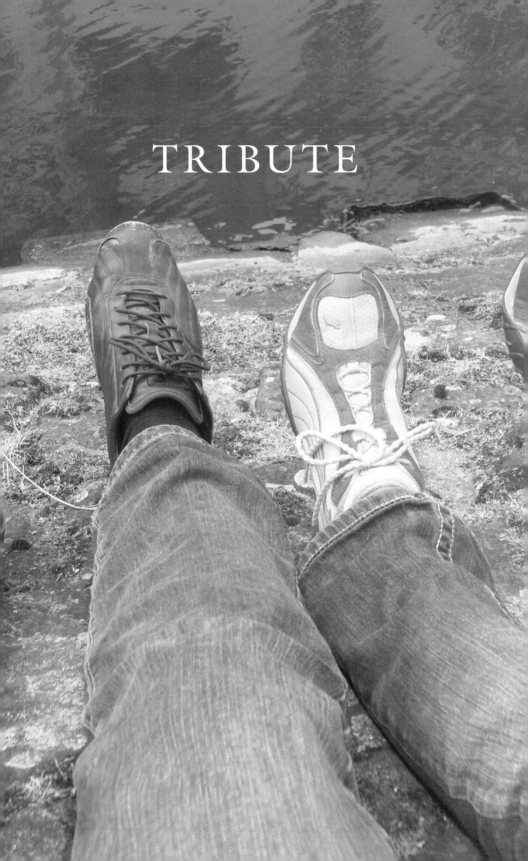

TRIBUTE

I needed to transition Kyle to a new day program. For lots of reasons, his current program was not meeting his needs, or mine. So, once again, I had to explore the difficult questions about what I wanted for Kyle, and where he belonged. I had to ask myself what better options existed, if any.

After an extensive search, I found a place I liked, yet still felt very cautious. I went through a lot of preliminaries to be sure this was a good fit for all of us. With what I learned, I made the decision to move Kyle to this new place, and planned a comprehensive staff training day so Kyle and his new team could get off to the best possible start.

I've often said I wish Kyle had shown up with a manual. Well, this time, he was going to. I decided to write the first edition of the *Kyle Manual*.

Initially, the task felt daunting. There were the basics – food allergies, routines, and bee sting allergies. But, that didn't seem like enough. How could I help the new staff begin to know and understand Kyle? Many people just don't "get" Kyle, and I wanted to help.

So, I decided to write this manual from Kyle's voice, from his perspective. It took a lot of time and soul searching to put my thoughts on paper. I thought about what Kyle might want people to know and understand, and attempted to decode his behavior and share my special young man. Five pages later, Kyle's essence and voice emerged within the confines of the written word. Unexpectedly, what began as the introduction to the manual evolved into a tribute to a young man who is often underestimated and misunderstood.

Here is an excerpt:

> *"I have autism. This makes me behave differently than most people. I also have other issues that go along with my autism; so many things are hard for me.*

*First, it is hard for me to communicate. I am not able to
speak or sign, and don't gesture very much to communicate.
Much of what I'd like to communicate is sort of stuck in me,
and I'm not able to get it out. Sometimes people think this
means I don't really understand what they are saying or
what's going on. While it's true that I miss things sometimes,
because they are said or happen so quickly, I really do
understand and notice a lot more of what's happening
around me than what it appears. It's really easy for people to
underestimate me because of this. Have you ever heard the
saying 'not being able to speak is not the same as not having
anything to say?' Well, it's true."*

The response was overwhelmingly positive. People who know
and love Kyle were moved. Others who help with his care found it
extremely useful and read it again and again. It was a great way to
kick off the training with Kyle's new team. Every person received his
or her own personal copy, complete with the five-page tribute at the
beginning. It turned out to be a gift to all who know Kyle, and those
who do not, but will be part of his future.

Kyle's Manual will always go with him. As he evolves, so will it.
And, I no longer have to wish I had one – I do.

Oxygen-Rich Tool

*Begin a tribute or introduction about your child. Quickly list some of
the things you would want someone to know who will be working with or
caring for your child. If your child is verbally limited, give your child a
voice. This reminds people there is a voice inside, even though they may not
hear the words. Your quick list can easily evolve into a narrative and be
written in five-minute sessions over time.*

THE HARD WAY

When I was younger, I remember my dad pointing out that I was doing it the hard way.

"Why are you doing that the hard way?" he would ask. "It would be much easier if you would ..."

I don't remember the easier ways, but I distinctly remember the message: doing something the hard way just might be a bad thing.

I suppose shopping with Kyle might be considered shopping the hard way. The grocery store is one of Kyle's learning laboratories. Many of his life lessons can be addressed in this venue. I spend as much or more time guiding and teaching, as I do choosing the items we are going to purchase.

In the grocery store, paper is a tremendous temptation for Kyle. Kyle likes paper. His self-stimulating activity of choice is to flap and crinkle a crisp piece of paper until it is limp. Flapping is stress relief, and sometimes, entertainment. Over the years it has become a very strong habit. He is drawn to paper when he feels uncertain, or stressed, or in need of some sensory input. Come to think of it, he is drawn to paper when paper is around. And, in the store, coupons are sticking out all over the aisles, just asking to be grabbed. Sale tags abound. Kyle is like a kid in a candy shop; he can't keep his hands, or his attention, away from these paper magnets.

So, last week, price tags called out to Kyle. He would stop every few feet and reach to grab one. I would gently remind him the paper must stay on the shelf. A few times, he snatched one before I could preempt the strike. This, then, became an opportunity to help him practice returning the paper to its spot.

As time went on, the dynamic evolved. Kyle began to pause in front of tags and point to them. This was his way of asking for one. When I told him he couldn't have one, he was able to move on without grabbing. Pointing soon evolved to looking longingly at the tags, thinking, and then choosing not to take one. We stopped frequently during this trip. There were many meaningful teaching and learning moments.

By the end of our time at the store, Kyle had shifted from impulsive to mindful. He was able to slow down, think, and control his actions. He was exercising his shifting and thinking muscles. He performed numerous repetitions to strengthen the weaker, less-connected areas of his brain. Would we have to repeat this lesson on subsequent trips? Probably. Like working out at a gym, frequency and consistency build strength.

I suppose I did shopping the hard way. But, I wonder, how did doing something the hard way get such a bad rap, anyway?

Oxygen-Rich Tool

The feelings of accomplishment we experience after navigating the more challenging sides of life's mountains are a definite high. Even if you don't make it to the top, there are always rewards for the attempt. Is there something in your life that merits doing it the hard way? Try it.

THE QUESTION

I was standing atop Lookout Mountain. The ring of pollution surrounding Phoenix literally took some of my breath away. I inhaled deeply, allowing the particulates to settle into my lungs and wondered if I was really deriving any physical benefit from outdoor exercise. On some days, perhaps the benefits were primarily psychological. That day, it turned out, I was really there for the serendipitous moment to follow.

Within minutes of stopping, a man joined me. When he discovered I was a "local," he began quizzing me about other area hikes. Our conversation evolved to the subject of age. I can still see the grin on his face when he proudly informed me he was eighty. He went on to say he could hardly believe he was that age. I commended him for his vigor and positive attitude. This man had a real spring to his step. "Once you say you're too old, it's over," he informed me. Now, there's a profound piece of wisdom. He beamed as he went on to share his adventures on Mt. Rainier.

At home, later that evening, I was sitting down to dinner with my family. It had been another brutal day in the stock market, and Neil, my husband, was completely drained. I sensed the dinner conversation might spiral downward, so I pulled out "the question."

"What was the best part of your day today?"

This is the question I have asked my daughters each night before our final goodnight kiss. Many times, it has been the key to turning our attitudes away from difficulty and toward gratitude.

"The best part of my day is happening right now," Neil shared. He was sitting at the table enjoying a home-cooked meal with his wife and son. When it was my turn, I remembered the man on the mountain. I could still see his smile and the sparkle in his eyes. I recalled his words of wisdom. The best part of my day was meeting him and receiving his powerful reminder.

The question. It brought us back to what was good. The dark clouds of the stock market lifted a little bit. In gratitude, we both relaxed.

Oxygen-Rich Tool

What was the best part of your day today? This is a powerful question, and a great way to wrap up the day, whether at the dinner table, or when saying your goodnights. It's all about noticing the good.

FOLD FORWARD

I sat down to write what I thought at the time was the last piece for this book. I felt enthusiastic, yet had a bit of trepidation. I wasn't quite sure how to approach this piece. I knew the tool I wanted to present, and had a vague idea of the story I wanted to share. A few scraps of paper scribbled with spur-of-the-moment ideas adorned my desk. Unfortunately, none of this was much help. The more I wrote, the less I connected with what I wanted to express. My mind became muddled and judgmental. I was stuck.

Before I knew it, it was time for my weekly piano lesson. I was having a hard time pulling myself away from the computer. I thought if I just stayed a bit longer and tried a little harder, the story would flow. Wrong. Okay, maybe I just need to stop for now. I left the computer, grabbed my music, and dashed out the door.

Going to my piano lesson turned out to be just what the doctor ordered. Allowing myself to be a student – make errors, receive correction, and work through the learning process – is both challenging and fun. I use other parts of my brain, and it feels really good. So, by the time I returned home, I was alert and recharged, and the words flowed through my fingers and onto the page.

There's something about getting out of my routine, or making an abrupt change in what I am doing, that is very powerful. Though I might resist at first, it is always helpful. Sometimes I need to jumpstart my creativity, or regain my patience with Kyle. Or, maybe I'm craving a little dose of mental or physical stillness, which is often difficult to find when living with autism.

I'm not always able to leave the house on the spur of the moment and head to the nearest nature spot or music lesson. So, what's a girl to do? Fold forward, for at least a minute.

This yoga pose is amazingly powerful in its simplicity. I bend over, folding from my hips, and reach toward the floor. I allow my head to hang loosely, relaxing my neck. My arms dangle, and my fingertips graze my ankles or the floor. Busyness and tension flow right out the top of my head.

The forward fold reverses my flow of energy and even allows me to see life from another perspective. I shake things up a bit, empty out, and step out of my routine. My search for stillness stops there. I've found it, at least for the moment. My energy and creativity are right behind.

Oxygen–Rich Tool

Fold forward. Fold from the hips rather than the waist. Breathe. With each inhalation, lift and lengthen the front torso slightly. With each exhalation, release a little more into the fold. There's no place to go. Simply be in this space and allow the mental busyness to flow right out the top of your head.

Warning: This pose has been known to calm the brain; relieve stress, mild anxiety, headache and insomnia; improve digestion; and reduce fatigue. Powerful stuff.

WORDS

I was visiting a potential day program for Kyle when I noticed the staff referred to the individuals who attended the program as "students." This was different. In most programs I'd experienced, they referred to them as consumers.

I like using the word, student. Aren't we all really lifelong students? I have learned my most significant lessons in the hands-on classroom of life. Why should it be any different for people with special needs?

Words might seem like small things, but they have the power to create a shift in vision, then attitude, then thoughts, then feelings, and then actions. Using the word, student, when referring to adults with special needs, reminds everyone to see them as such. It sets the tone for an entire program, and is a powerful reminder that the staff is here to teach, and the individuals are here to learn.

I'm working diligently on finishing this book. I told myself I "have to" write today. I noticed that thinking "have to" added an element of pressure, and might even make writing feel like a burden. Do I really want to feel pressured into doing one of the things I love to do? What if I change one word? I "choose" to write today. Now, the flavor and feeling are completely different. I am making a decision. Changing the word again, I "get" to write today. Now, writing becomes a privilege. I get to write today. How lucky I am.

By changing one word, writing morphs from burden to privilege. That's pretty powerful. The words we think, and the words we say out loud, set the tone for how we view a person, a project, and even a day program.

I like seeing Kyle as a student. And, I like that the people he may be with all day see him as a student, too. They might just see their role as teacher, guide or coach, rather than caregiver or sitter. That makes a big difference.

Oxygen-Rich Tool

Change your words and change your thoughts, you change your attitude. Notice a word, any word that might not serve you well. Change it. It makes a big difference.

MUSIC MAGIC

I'm learning your favorites,
I'm learning you
What you'll order for dinner,
Your favorite ice cream too . . . I'm learning youuuu.

These days, this song is one of my favorites. My daughter, Leah, sings this delightful piece as she plays it on her acoustic guitar. Her sweet voice, wise lyrics, and gentle accompaniment are literally music to my ears. As her mother, I'm not at all biased, either. Kyle loves this song, too. In fact, I believe he has a special place in his heart for his sister's music.

Music has such a simple and powerful impact on my life. It is my mood changer, working its magic on my many moods, which seem to blow in and out of my day like the wind.

It's only in recent years I've noticed the full impact music has on Kyle. Music is Kyle's elixir of choice. Each day, I observe how his mannerisms and mood appear to shift on a dime depending on the type of music playing. When he came home upset the other day, music by Enya helped create an immediate shift. Last night in the car, it took only a few seconds for him to shift from vocalizing with an agitated tone, to happily singing along with the bluegrass music playing on the radio.

Personally, if it's available, I often enjoy quiet. Perhaps that's because it was such a rare commodity in our home for many years. However, if I'm feeling a little down, I know where to go. Leah Nobel's song, *Favorites,* tops my favorites playlist. Just a few seconds in, and *Favorites* works its magic on me.

Oxygen-Rich Tool

Take the time to enjoy some of your favorite music. It's an easy, almost effortless way to create a mood shift, and make life a little sweeter.

ROUTINES

Routines. They might not be exciting, but sometimes a routine is just what we need.

Today, one of our routines got us through the morning. I stayed up too late last night. Kyle got up extra early. This was a recipe for exhaustion. I was ready for bed before I even got out of it. Thank goodness for my "get Kyle ready for his day" routine. We do virtually the same thing each time. I've got this routine down to a science so I can get him out the door in time for his morning ride. I do it without really having to think.

The downside is that Kyle doesn't have to think, either. This is why, on most days, I try to tweak it, mix it up a little, and make the routine more dynamic, more similar to the world in which we live. I might do something as simple as moving his toothpaste to a different shelf in the medicine cabinet. Kyle has to think, thereby using a different part of his brain to process the situation and respond. He has to live a little less on autopilot, even if for just a moment.

Making Kyle's world more dynamic, even in small ways, requires me to think as well. I enjoy the challenge of coming up with ways to shake up his world so he can then tackle his challenges. When he is tackling, he is growing. I like that.

Today, however, was not one of those times. I was tired, and I needed to acknowledge that. I was ever so grateful for our morning routine. No cerebral dancing required on my part, or on Kyle's. And, it was okay. In fact, it felt really good. I think I am growing too!

Oxygen-Rich Tool

Without routines, we would have to "think" every time we started our car. Then again, if we were always operating on autopilot, we might not know what to do when it didn't start!

Today, notice when you are in a routine. Take a moment to appreciate your routine and the way it serves you. Nothing to do, fix or change. Just notice and appreciate.

I love writing, yet there are many times when I have a hard time getting started. I can find a million things to do other than write, but once I get going, I get lost in the writing experience. It is my passion and I truly enjoy it.

I enjoy helping Kyle learn and experience more of the world. Still, there are many times when I find it difficult to get started. I get stuck in the proverbial mud, even though I love the rewards of working with Kyle – a moment of connection, a small accomplishment, a new understanding about each of us.

One of my newest passions is playing the piano. When I practice, I am instantly transported to the present moment. I love it. I enjoy the challenge. Playing is therapy for me. And yet, again, I often find it difficult to get myself to practice consistently. I put it off. I distract myself with other things.

I am passionate about my writing, my son, and my music. I'm not sure why I procrastinate with the very things I enjoy doing. Behavior doesn't always follow a logical path, does it?

My solution: JUST SHOW UP! This is the mantra I use to propel myself into action. I don't remember when I first became aware of this mantra, but I've seen it work over and over again. The best way to overcome my inner resistance is to show up. Show up at the page, with my son, or at the piano. The rest seems to take care of itself, in some form or another.

I resisted writing today, but I decided to show up at the blank computer screen anyway. Before I knew it, there were words on the page, in some form or another.

Oxygen-Rich Tool

Can't get going? Don't know how you are going to accomplish something? Show up. Choose an intention and begin by showing up for it. The rest will unfold, in some form or another.

NOTICE

We had just finished a very strenuous posture in yoga class. For simplicity's sake, I will call it pretzel-twist-asana. Though extremely challenging, the intensity felt good, almost as if I was squeezing the toxins right out of my body. It felt even better when we stopped.

Soon, we would do unto the other side, but for a few moments, we had a reprieve. We were asked to step to the top of our mats and pause. The blood flowed back into those areas of my body that had been compressed. I felt warm and tingly.

One of the things I love about yoga is when we stop and check in with ourselves between postures. We pause, breathe, feel, and notice. There's no hurry to move on to the next thing – nothing to fix or do. We simply listen and notice what's happening in our body and mind. No analysis or judgment is necessary, just pure observation, sensation and surrender.

I now get that the lessons in yoga are the lessons of life. When I remember, I use them. The days are so packed with have to's, need to's, and want to's, I often feel as if there is no breathing room, no pausing space, and too little time.

Last week, Kyle and I were rushing so he could be ready on time. Actually, I was rushing and Kyle was having no part of it. Rushing and autism do not go together very well. He was unfocused and squiggly, and just wasn't cooperating. As much as I tried to convince him to settle down, he couldn't.

Eventually, remembering my yoga lesson, I stopped. I took a breath and checked in. I was a bit worked up. In essence, I was mirroring Kyle. I stood still for a few moments, watching and noticing. He was having such a good time doing his autism dance. I, on the other hand, was feeling a bit stressed. I spent a few more moments in pause mode and took another deep breath. Kyle kept moving. Then, something subtle happened. In the pause, I decided to calm down.

Instead of trying to change what was happening, I decided to make his breakfast while he did his thing.

Guess what? We somehow managed to get it all done. We were late, but in the scheme of things, what did it really matter?

Oxygen-Rich Tool

Take a short break. Check in with yourself. Notice your thoughts. What is your attitude? What does your body feel like? What are you doing? Just stop, breathe, listen, and feel. Where you are is where you are.

LIVE NOW

Slowly but surely, I am transferring our home videos to DVD. The process is simple and painless, but every time I get involved in the project, I feel compelled to meander down memory lane.

One of our videos starts with Kyle, age eleven, agitated and at the height of one of his severe anxiety episodes. I'm not really sure why we recorded this. The scene quickly jumps to Rachel and Leah frolicking joyfully in the backyard. I hope they were as happy as they appeared. When the scene changes again, I am standing by a pale-turquoise lake with snowcapped peaks in the background.

Neil and I had taken a trip to Canada. It was one of the few "just the two of us" vacations we took after our children were born and was, therefore, very special. There we were, smiling and enjoying ourselves in the incredible Canadian Rockies, just one month after Kyle's severe anxiety episode.

I was surprised to see the date. Yes, we had planned this trip long in advance. I don't remember if we hesitated going when we encountered rough times with Kyle. I know I had a lot of confidence in Christy, our support person at the time, and the one who would be taking care of Kyle. She had been with Kyle for many years and had experienced his most difficult times. She could certainly have handled anything that came up.

So, Neil and I did what some might think was unthinkable – we took a vacation. We left the country knowing Kyle might experience rough times while we were away. I recall feeling intensely hurt at that time. But, for a week, I chose to set that aside to have a life away from worry and angst. We allowed ourselves the guilty pleasure of living one of our dreams. The timing wasn't optimal; in fact, it was lousy. But, we made a choice. We chose to live now.

What we didn't know then was that this was the beginning of an eleven-year period of debilitating, cyclical, anxiety episodes with Kyle.

This was a difficult period for our family on all levels. I'm grateful for the time I had with my husband. We both needed it to fortify us for the rough journey ahead. In hindsight, had we waited for better days, we would have waited a very long time.

Live now.

Oxygen-Rich Tool

What is it you are waiting to do until your child is "better"? Make a quick list of "live now" activities or adventures. Maybe it's an evening out, or simply curling up with a good book. Perhaps it's an overnight travel adventure. Take one small action step toward making it a reality.

GRATEFULNESS

It had been a rough evening with Kyle. He was on an "energy high." Perhaps someone spiked his water with Red Bull.

Kyle's energy highs show up as an insatiable need for movement. We took a long walk-run in the neighborhood. That wasn't enough. He walked and ran on the treadmill until he was splashing in sweat puddles. Phew! Thank goodness that calmed him down. For two minutes, that is. He popped up to rearrange the dining chairs and run a few laps around the kitchen island. He did several sets of this. After a session on the weight machine, and a five-minute chug of ice water, Kyle began to wind down, and eventually crashed.

It was time for me to make an attempt at winding down, too. My upholstered chaise was inviting me to climb aboard and relax. I jumped at the invitation. I noticed my gratitude journal sitting in the basket beside me. Was that a layer of dust on the colorful, recycled-paper cover? Sure enough, it was. The book was calling to me, but honestly, I didn't know if I had the energy to pick it up.

Certainly, I could use a little dose of my own inspiration right now. I cracked it open. The last recorded entry was six weeks ago. Oops. My nightly ritual had gone by the wayside, forgotten. I began to skim through it, and before I knew it my pen was in hand.

What could I possibly be grateful for right now? My son had just worn me down to a frazzle. Of course, there is always my health, which is too easily taken for granted. And, I was able to keep up with him, wasn't I? I wrote, "I am grateful that this evening is over. Now, I get to go to sleep and start a brand new day tomorrow."

I have been using a gratitude journal for a long time. It's been one of the simplest and most useful tools I know to support and encourage feeling good. Recently, I became aware of some research on the value of cultivating gratitude, and keeping a gratitude journal is at the top of the list. Imagine that!

In *Thanks: How The New Science of Gratitude Can Make You Happier*, Robert Emmons, Ph.D., writes, "The technique of recording the blessings you are grateful for makes people happier. By writing each day, we magnify and expand upon the sources of goodness in our lives."

Emmons compared a group that made a weekly list of five things for which they were grateful, to a group that made a weekly list of five hassles or things that irritated them. Participants in the grateful group were 25 percent happier! They felt better about their lives as a whole, felt more optimistic about the future, and even spent more time exercising and experienced fewer physical illness symptoms than did the hassles group. Now, that's impressive. Sign me up.

I brushed the dust off the cover, and with pen in hand, decided to recommit to my nightly practice of writing in my gratitude journal.

Oxygen-Rich Tool

Join me. List five things you are grateful for each day. That's it!

Not feeling it? Do it anyway, and the feelings will follow. If you want, make it special by buying an attractive journal. A good-looking book will help invite and inspire you.

This ritual works. Particularly when you do it. Wink.

NEXT ACTIONS

Here we are again, at another fork in the road.

Things had been going along fairly smoothly with Kyle's day program when, suddenly, a major upheaval occurred. Things quickly spiraled into chaos. Kyle would need to leave his day program, again. Didn't we just do this eight months ago? Like it or not, we were going to do it again.

"Change is good," so the saying goes. Most of the time, I agree. I look back and see change as a blessing. So, why doesn't it feel so good at first? I suppose it's because change can be scary. It's easy to get comfortable with the status quo. Now, we are venturing forth into the unknown.

Over the years, one of my biggest challenges has been keeping an ongoing, high-quality support system in place. Good support lightens my load. At the same time, finding, training, and maintaining that support also adds to my load. It has felt, at times, harder than living with autism.

Our family has been very fortunate in that we've worked with some really great programs, and some really great people. We've also had times when we could not find a good fit for Kyle. And this is what I am facing once again. Another search, and another change. Sigh. I feel overwhelmed and a little fearful. I have been known to fret, worry, and panic, especially when it comes to Kyle's quality of life.

So, I decided to try a different approach. I decided to focus on my next action. What do I need to do to move forward? Realistically, if I want to make a change in this situation, it will happen only through my deliberate action. In this case, I decided to take one action at a time until I achieved my desired result – a new day program for Kyle.

My first action was to make a phone call. Then another. Then another. Since the rest of the world did not have the same sense of urgency, I had to be very patient. Sometimes my next action was simply to wait calmly for someone to respond.

With each call, I took a step forward and felt more empowered. As a bonus, I also felt supported by the people who were trying to help.

Within a reasonable amount of time, I found a new program for Kyle. To add icing to the cake, his personal aide decided to make the move with him. I felt lucky. While there are no guarantees, this new program was a step up. We had a brand new starting point from which to move forward.

Thinking up my next action and taking it was kind of fun. Though the outcome was out of my control, I felt a sense of personal power and control. One action at a time felt good.

Oxygen-Rich Tool

Trying to create a change? What is the next action you can take to move forward, even if it's just a baby step? Decide and do it. One action at a time will propel you to the next.

P.S. Sometimes the next action might be deciding not to take an action.

BREATHE NOW,
AND BE WITH
WHAT IS

Stop, just for this moment, and take a deep breath. Breathe deeply, filling your belly as well as your lungs. Count as you breathe in. Count as you breathe out. Breathe in and out for the same number of counts. Do this for as long as you can. Even just a minute can make a difference, as it did this morning.

I arrived at the top of the mountain and soaked up the 360-degree view of the desert valley around me. I sat in a shady spot and enjoyed the slight breeze and my bottle of ice water. Unlike most mornings, I even had some extra time to contemplate.

One phrase kept showing up in my mind: be with what is.

I took a deep breath and let it out with a long, loud sigh. I noticed how easy it felt to "be with what is" when life was going my way. I was in a good mood and had a slice of quiet time to jumpstart my day.

My thoughts drifted to my friend, Kathy, and her family. They are going through a very rough period with Mark. His seizures were finally under control, but now his medication is causing some extreme, unwanted side effects. Seizures have been replaced with agitation.

Be with what is.

You've got to be kidding, right? Does it even apply in this situation? Yes. More than ever. In fact, it is essential. We are all praying for a change so Mark and his family can return to a more peaceful state. In the meantime, what remains is what it is.

For me, "be with what is" often seems elusive when I'm trying to get through a day when Kyle's special needs send challenges my way. How do I incorporate this wisdom? Is there a bridge from struggle to being with what is?

I had an opportunity to test this out this morning. We were running late and Kyle was moving at a snail's pace. I didn't have time for anything extra. However, I realized I had to breathe anyway. So, as I did at the top of the mountain, I took a deep breath and let it out with a very loud sigh. It felt so good, I did it a few more times. The situation didn't change, but at least for a moment, taking a deep breath served as a stepping stone out of the place of resistance and into being with what is.

Oxygen-Rich Tool

Take a deep breath. Fill yourself with air from your belly up to the tips of your lungs. Hold it for a second or two. Then release it through the mouth with an audible sigh. Repeat as many times as you can, and for the moment, be with what is.

SHIFT

All we needed was dish soap and toilet paper. Typically, that's an errand most people can accomplish with a dash to the store.

Last night, I decided the "dish soap/toilet paper errand" would be the perfect way to end the evening. Kyle and I had plenty of time, so I set my intention. My goal was to slow down the shopping experience so Kyle could have a competent role in the process.

At first, Kyle froze at the front door, completely blocking the doorway. When I convinced him to walk in, he made a grand entrance. He became a racecar driver with the shopping cart. He moved at almost a dead run and began vocalizing, the volume of his deep voice escalating. Kyle may not be verbal in words, but his vocalizations announced loud and clear that he was now in the store. All eyes were on us.

What about my intention to slow this experience way down? My first instinct was to race through the store with him, find the things we needed, and get the heck outta there! We could be in and out in less than five. In all honesty, my other instinct was to turn around and leave immediately.

Then I remembered why I had chosen to bring Kyle in the first place. It wasn't just about the toilet paper. We were here so he could practice "being" at the store. That meant he needed to come down a few notches from his frenzied entry. He needed to downshift so he could process at his own speed. Then, he'd at least have the chance to participate mindfully in the shopping experience.

Each time Kyle makes a shift, he strengthens those shifting muscles in his brain. Slowing down offers him this opportunity. Due to his autism, he processes at a much slower speed than the typical person. Slowing down offers him a chance to process. As he processes, he can participate. Slowing down offers him the possibility of having a competent role, whatever that might be.

So, I stopped myself just as I was about to shift into survival mode. I slowed down so I could be there as Kyle's guide. I knew slowing down would have to begin with me.

We pulled over. Kyle was like a horse at the starting gate ready to take off. I insisted he "just stop." My intention was to stand there for as long as it would take for him to downshift.

I said nothing, and I did nothing. After a while, we were two people standing still, silently staring at the packages of toilet paper. A shift had taken place. I remembered to breathe again.

Slowing down was my gift to Kyle that evening. It was also my gift to myself. The gift was in the shift.

Oxygen-Rich Tool

Give yourself the gift of the shift. Practice the art of slowing down with someone who would really benefit from your intention and effort. Maybe that someone is you.

LAUGH

We laughed until our faces hurt. I don't know if I have ever laughed as hard or as much in such a short period of time as I did last Saturday when we went to a live performance by the comedian, Jim Gaffigan. Jim takes ordinary living and makes it funny. Bowling, eating food, emptying the trash – these ordinary parts of daily life are all churned into fodder for humor.

Jim Gaffigan transforms life into comedy.

Laughter is essential – it's a sanity saver. It's simple. It's free. It's something everyone can do. But, perhaps most importantly, it helps us change our attitude about whatever might be happening in our lives. We can laugh at the absurdity, or the uncertainty, or the sheer nonsensical nature of it all. We can laugh at life, and with life. It helps us transform life into comedy.

Laughter connects us to each other. It's a universal language. The first time a baby laughs is a priceless moment. There's something about a young infant's toothless grin and deep belly laugh that makes everyone smile.

Laughter is contagious. Kyle, who has difficulty with the nuances of language, often joins us in laughter. He may not get the joke, but he gets laughing. A good cry can be turned into a good laugh with the help of the right person. Laughter is magical in that way.

So why is it some days go by and I don't laugh? Partly because laughter doesn't come as easily when you work alone most of the day. Mostly it's because I have an advanced degree in taking life too seriously.

Fortunately for my family and me, we live with a man who can easily revert to the age of ten with his corny jokes, accents, and overall silliness. My husband injects a dose of humor and laughter into our lives on a regular basis. He helps make living with autism, and just plain living, both fun and funny.

I've always heard that laughter is good medicine. That's very true. But, sometimes I forget to take mine. That is, until my husband comes home. Jim Gaffigan, Neil Nobel – I can't help but laugh!

Oxygen-Rich Tool

Did you laugh today? This week? This month? Indulge in a simple sanity saver. Find humor in the ordinary. Joke with your family and friends. Read something funny. Listen to a comedian. Laugh about life. Just laugh.

ASK

As we crossed the finish line, my soul smiled. We were greeted by a sea of people all wearing bright-red *It's All About Attitude* shirts, applauding and cheering loudly. Once again, we had completed the annual Phoenix Zoowalk to raise awareness and money for autism.

Each year, Kyle's therapist, Kim, forms a team to support the autism cause and honor Kyle. Admittedly, I usually feel reserved about asking people to attend. It starts very early in the morning, and for many of them, it's a long drive. I also feel awkward asking people to donate money, even to a worthy cause. I don't want them to feel obligated.

This year, Kim and I decided to invite the staff of Kyle's day program to join our team. Though he'd only been there a few months, we had formed a connection with them. We were completely unprepared for the overwhelming response. Not only did the entire staff decide to attend, but they also brought their extended families. People who didn't know Kyle, and perhaps weren't even familiar with autism, turned out to show their support. I was deeply touched.

One of my biggest challenges on this journey has been to ask for help and support. Though hundreds of people have crossed my threshold during Kyle's twenty-four years, I have never found it easy to ask. There have been times when I wanted to crawl into my cave and shut the door because I felt so fearful and discouraged. My independent streak would rear its head and tell me, "I can climb this mountain by myself!"

Sorry independent streak, that's not true. Support has been essential to having balance in my life. It lightens my load, and by doing that, I'm better able to carry my load.

When I ask for help, I offer others the opportunity to give. Giving is powerful stuff. By giving, people receive directly, or indirectly, the perspective and insights that come from knowing Kyle. As a bonus, I help to create a compassionate community, and a special network of support for Kyle and our family.

Did I *need* thirty-five people to join Kyle's team at the Zoowalk? No. Was seeing everyone show up in red "superhero" *Attitude* shirts the best gift of the entire weekend? Most definitely.

Oxygen-Rich Tool

Ask. Want some help or support? Someone to help teach or care for your child, help with housework, be part of your team, listen, or hold your hand during rough times? Ask, and you may receive. No guarantees, but asking is a great first step.

FAST FIX

Kyle needed to be measured for an extension on his medical ID bracelet. This had been a nagging errand on my to-do list for far too long. He was in a mellow mood, so I thought it was an ideal day to go to the Fast Fix jewelry store at the mall.

I was unprepared for how busy the mall was on a Saturday. We entered near the food court – the noisiest, most crowded part of the entire mall, and the farthest from our destination. I remembered why we never go there on the weekend. Just a foot inside the door, Kyle stopped. He put his arm around me for reassurance and indicated he wanted to leave. I convinced myself, and him, that it was best for us to stay and complete our errand.

Panic started building in Kyle as we made the slow trek to the other end of the mall. When we saw the long line at the jewelry store, we decided to detour into Sears so dad could buy a power tool, and Kyle could calm down.

Then, suddenly, as we entered Sears, Kyle gripped me in a bear hug. Panic! Kyle hugs when he gets scared, and this was one of the most powerful hugs in the history of scared bear hugs. When he was small, he would be up in my arms. Now, at six feet tall, I thought I would soon be up in HIS arms.

How do you help a young man with autism when he's so frightened he can't let go? I let him hug me for a long time. Right there at the entrance to Sears. I breathed deeply to calm myself, and with hopes of transferring some of that calmness to Kyle. I reassured him he was going to be okay.

Once he calmed down, we walked farther into the store, only to repeat the hug scenario all over again when he panicked in the sporting goods section. Thank goodness for the nearby outdoor furniture area where we were able to sit down and catch our breath.

Several bear hugs and one drill purchase later, we had made our way back to the jewelry store. After Kyle was measured, he waited outside with Dad as I took care of the remaining business. This was going to take at least an hour. So much for a fast fix.

When I rejoined my family, I noticed sweat dripping down the side of Kyle's face. He was standing still, but that feeling of sheer panic was evident on his face, and was soaking the back of his shirt. At that moment, I became acutely aware of what Kyle must experience at the mall – sensory overload at its finest.

While I might wish for a fast fix, at times the best I can do is be there to support and reassure Kyle. Sometimes this means simply allowing him to hold on tight while I remain calm. I remind myself that we will be okay. This too shall pass.

Oxygen-Rich Tool

In real life, there usually aren't any fast fixes. Practice the art of being there for someone. What does being there look and feel like? How about not worrying about the time or what other people think, being patient, and doing whatever it takes to help the person through the situation? Do you know someone who could use your support?

GRATITUDE
IN ACTION

Gratitude is one of *the* most profound keys to peace, good feelings, and happiness. Gratitude *in action* bumps it up a few notches. Taking a moment to express your gratitude to someone who makes a difference in the life of your loved one, and therefore yours, is a small, yet profoundly significant act.

Dear Rich and Kathleen:

Every week, I drive across town so Kyle can experience music therapy with both of you. Kyle shows up differently each time. No matter how he shows up, you welcome him with music and loving arms. The slate is clean. He might be wild, he might be calm. You begin with him where he is and go from there. You offer him a competent role within your special musical trio. Often, this does not come easily for Kyle.

There is a delicate dance of give and take between the three of you. Wanting him to initiate, to participate independently, you wait, but not so long you lose him completely. You guide, but not too much, working through his resistance, and respecting his resistance. There are no rules – just your judgment and instincts to rely on. Somehow, the end result is always music to my ears. Some sessions are magical; others, challenging.

When I come in at the end of the session, you manage to pick out the good. The focus is on what he did, rather than what he didn't do. That attitude permeates all your sessions with Kyle. You often share thoughtful insights of understanding. We still, after all this time, have questions for each other. I can't always hear the musical magic that takes place, so you educate me. Excellence lies in the details.

We all have the same intention of helping Kyle be the best he can be – to add richness to his quality of life. We are a team, and a good one, at that.

> With deep appreciation,
> Gayle, Kyle's mom

Dear Kim:

From the moment we walked in the door, Kyle was visibly delighted to be at the restaurant. He shuddered soundlessly, holding it in, keeping it together. He has learned to control the screams of pleasure he voices freely at home.

Using his straw ever so gently, he delicately sipped his drink. He waited patiently for the food to arrive, and even ate slowly. He looked around, taking in the surroundings, and then shifted his gaze to the side – to you, his guide and friend.

If you had asked me just a few years ago whether I could visualize this moment in Kyle's future, it might have been difficult to picture. He did not function so well in restaurants, where certain behavior is expected. This is another one of those Kyle miracles.

I recognize it took several years of your patient guidance and coaching, each week, believing in Kyle and wanting to offer him the experience of dining out. Some weeks were not easy, but you persevered through those difficult moments.

Last night, as Neil and I sat across from our son, at his best, in the booth of a restaurant, we marveled at the outcome of your hard work and dedication.

> With gratitude,
> Gayle and Neil, Kyle's proud parents

Oxygen-Rich Tool

Jot down a short letter of appreciation. Use email, snail mail, poster board, or post-it note. It all works. Feels good for you, feels good for the recipient.

FEELING GOOD

I hike. It's one of the primary ways I mainline endorphins, the feel-good substances that flood the brain as a result of a good workout. Plus, I really enjoy it.

There are times, though, that it's hard for me to get going, especially if the morning with Kyle has been hectic. This morning, I needed some help, so I invited an invisible hand to push me out the door (another way I motivate myself). I took a deep breath. The air was perfect – not yet hot. In fact, there was just a touch of coolness to it, which is always encouraging at the end of April in Phoenix.

As I began walking, I noticed how sluggish I felt. It was a little hard to put one foot in front of the other. Usually this feeling dissipates after I get warmed up. Not today. I felt as if I were crawling to the top of the mountain. My mental chatter about why was pretty loud, too. It was almost enough to ruin the trip.

Eventually, however, I made it to the top. I did it. The feel-good stuff kicked in. Fortunately, it's not affected by mental chitchat, or by how sluggish I am on the trek to the top. So, feeling exhilarated, I took a few deep breaths, released the remaining dialogue from my mind, and smiled. The journey down was going to be a piece of cake. Speaking of cake, I'll take chocolate, of course, because there's always room for more feel-good boosters.

Oxygen-Rich Tool

What boosts your endorphin level? How do you help yourself feel good? What creates a positive shift in your mental and emotional energy? Gift yourself with a small slice of time and do what it takes. Yes, chocolate counts too.

BALANCE

For a moment, I stood gracefully in dancer's pose this morning. Focusing my gaze on a spot on the floor in front of me, I grasped my foot behind me and stood perfectly still as I extended my other hand into the air. Ahh, now I felt graceful and balanced like a dancer. But, it wasn't long before I began to wobble. With each wobble, my standing foot worked harder to make tiny adjustments to stabilize my body.

Wild arm-waving, wobbling, falling out – whether we're talking about yoga, or life, balance is not really a place to which we arrive, but more a matter of readjustments.

Having a son with autism has made this balance business extra tricky for me. When my children were younger, it often felt like a real struggle. I thought balance was a destination. I believed one day I might actually attain balance in my life. I would spend just the right amount of time working with my son, playing with and caring for my small daughters, and having "me time." If my life was *really* balanced, I might even have time for my husband.

Through yoga, and having lived an extra twenty years since my children were small, I think I finally understand balance. Balance is a process. I set my sight on where I'd like to be. I make an attempt. I wobble. I get back on track. I wobble a lot and fall out completely. I make modifications, or even go for a complete change of direction. I begin again with the full knowledge that I might be readjusting all over again. Sometimes, I even rest and dare to do nothing.

The kids are young adults now. My son still has autism. I am still seeking balance. I continue to wobble a lot. That is part of the journey. Just knowing that, I feel kind of, um, balanced.

Oxygen-Rich Tool

Seeking balance? Let yourself wobble today. Stand on one foot for a full minute. Switch to the other foot. Not wobbling yet? Try it on a pillow. If you lose your balance, simply readjust and start over.

Got kids? Invite them to play with you. They probably won't have any judgments about wobbling and falling out. For them, it's all part of the fun.

RESILIENCE

$Late$ the other night, I was sitting upstairs when I heard the sweet sounds of my college-age daughter and her two friends coming from the family room downstairs. They were boisterously talking and laughing, and from the snippets of conversation that floated up my way, I realized they had found the old bin of "dress up" clothes. The girls were having a blast taking photos of themselves in outrageous get-ups. Simple fun.

It was hard to believe that just four days prior, my daughter had been in the depths of despair.

Resilience.

Each day since then, I had observed her process of bouncing back – going out, spending time with friends, joking, singing, and speaking in accents. When the accents appeared, I knew for certain she was feeling better. But I wonder, does it just seem to flow and happen automatically, or does she work at it?

I don't know. What I notice is that, little by little, she manages to creep out of her gloom and reemerge, a little stronger, hopefully wiser.

Resilience. The word itself sounds delicious. What an amazing and beautiful process.

Oxygen-Rich Tool

Take notice. Pay attention. Can you see examples of your resilience sprinkled throughout the day? How about throughout your life? What do you do to lift yourself up when you're feeling down? Observe a child. They are often incredibly adept at bouncing back, and therefore beautifully resilient.

PAGES

My mind is an amazing creature. It can take one thought or concern and completely run amok with it.

Here's how it works: I start thinking about the future. I am older, my husband is older, my daughters are older, Kyle is older. Oh no! What will happen when Kyle is older? Where will he live? Who will take care of him? I mean, who will REALLY take care of him? Who will love him? Who will be there for him? Who will advocate for him? What if he ends up in an awful place? I picture that and I shudder. I can NEVER let that happen. How can I keep that from happening?

On and on it goes. Worry, worry, and more worry. Now I have a knot in the pit of my stomach, and my heart feels heavy. My mind can't stop creating scenarios and worrying about them. Pretty soon, I'm really upset. This could easily ruin an entire day if I allow it.

I sense this is a familiar scenario for most human beings. As parents, I know we all worry about the future, especially as it relates to our children. When a child has special needs and requires a lot of support, that worry feels greater. What's a mother to do? I can look for a solution, and sometimes I do. I also can dig into my toolbox and pull out the pages. I can set pen to paper and just start writing.

Writing is freeing. I put pen to paper and write what is on my mind until I have filled up the page. I just keep the pen moving. If time permits, I write three pages, but one works really well, too. This isn't the pretty journal type of writing, but the messy "write whatever spills out of my mind" type. In fact, I purposely write in a plain notebook, rather than a decorative journal. Then, I feel free to be messy, and whiny, and brutally honest with myself.

Once I'm done, I rarely reread what I've written, and usually discard the notebook when it's full. It's served its purpose. I often experience a release as a result of writing. I am able to move on, or let go, or take a necessary action. I feel refreshed and experience a shift in my attitude. Sometimes this process jumpstarts my creativity, or I end up solving a problem.

Spilling my guts out on paper is extremely therapeutic. Guts look so much better laid out on the page than spinning around in my head and making me crazy. I write, I dust myself off, and I move forward, ready to take the next step.

Oxygen-Rich Tool

Grab your pen. Write one page of whatever comes into your head. Keep the pen moving and let the thoughts fly without judgments or editing. The cost is small and the payoffs are large. Writing helps. Writing heals.

SILENCE

Last night, we sat on the stone wall in front of our house. This is one of Kyle's favorite places to sit after taking a walk, and part of our regular routine. We take in the night air, the moon, and the scent of the fragrant desert plants. We also take in each other. I might make an occasional comment, and Kyle, an occasional sound, but nearly always, we sit in silence.

There is space in the silence. In this space, I notice. I notice my son, and how much he enjoys the simple things in life. I notice his reactions, and his thinking moments, which can be subtle and easily missed. I feel the strong connection between us. I am reminded that to connect with another person is not just about the words that go back and forth. Connection is the unspoken, invisible part of the relationship between two people. It lives in the body language, facial expression, attitude, and, most importantly, the way those people intertwine in the dance that is a relationship.

It's taken me a long time to fully appreciate these moments of silence. I've had to learn to turn off the voices in my head that tell me I "should" be doing something more, like using this as a teachable moment. The list of things I should be doing is endless. Should be, should be, should be. It's also a distraction, because it diverts my attention from the moment, from what is.

I hear Kyle's heart and soul in the sound of the silence between us. As the artist, Allison Krauss, sings so beautifully, "you say it best, when you say nothing at all."

Oxygen-Rich Tool

Savor the silence with your child, or someone else you love. What do you notice? What do hear in the silence?

113

QUOTES

My daughters, Rachel and Leah, have gone back to college. Though not completely empty, their rooms feel like shells. Most of the important stuff has been taken. Thankfully, their scents – a mixture of fragrant cologne and sweet, delicious candles – still linger.

I miss them. I tiptoe into their rooms and see the childhood books that line the shelves. I wonder where the time has gone. A few inspirational quotations are still scattered around the room here and there. I love reading what speaks to my daughters. It's a different way of knowing them.

I confess, I'm a sucker for quotes. I have a piece of paper posted where I see it almost every day. It reads: "There are two ways to live your life. One is as though nothing is a miracle. The other is as though everything is a miracle."

Reading this quotation, I am transported to a place of gratitude. Thank you, Albert Einstein.

Quotations are inspiring. Like my daughters, I collect quotes that move me. They make great décor for the front of the refrigerator, my desk, or my computer screen. Sometimes, I shove them in a drawer or a book, only to discover them later.

I've found that quotes can inspire me to shift my attitude, just like that, right there in the moment. They are fantastic reminders about gratitude.

Quotes make me laugh. Sometimes they bring tears to my eyes. Quotes make me think, and remind me of what is truly important when I get off track. Sometimes they offer quick fixes. Quotes remind me to slow down. They also help put autism in perspective.

Here's one: "Experiencing life with those in the world of autism gives us a different lens, lending a new vision to everything we took for granted and hurried past on the way to notions of life's greater priorities." *Souls*, by Sharon Rosenbloom.

And finally, some of the best quotes seem to come from "unknown:" "We do not remember days, we remember moments." Thank you, unknown.

At the end of the day, quotes help me heal.

Oxygen-Rich Tool

Reading a quote is an awesome quick fix. Notice when quotes speak to you. Write them down. Type them out. Post them on your mirror, bulletin board, or refrigerator. Share them.

NOTHING

Sometimes I feel as if my mind is running 100 mph into the future, and my body is racing right alongside it, struggling to keep up.

Like many parents, I worry about what will happen to Kyle when I am no longer here. I still feel insecure about whether I am doing enough, or even doing the right things, whatever that means. Some days, my to-do list goes on and on. I find it difficult to quiet my mind enough to even slow down, let alone stop for a moment so I can catch my breath.

A few years ago, I asked my yoga instructor what one pose she recommended I do if I had a limited amount of time, yet wanted to squeeze some yoga into my day. I thought she'd recommend something for my back, or a pose that would be energizing. She was silent for a few moments and then said, "savasana."

The corpse pose? Where you lie down and do nothing? Nothing? Who has time for that? Reading my mind, she looked at me. I realized that was exactly the point. If I was going to thrive on this marathon, not just survive, I had to stop sprinting once in a while and take a break. Often, this is the last thing I think I have time for. So, I do it. This is a powerful reminder. Sometimes, doing nothing is the best thing we can do.

Oxygen-Rich Tool

You deserve a break today. Give yourself five minutes to take the savasana pose. If you do not have carpet, place a mat or folded blanket on the floor. Lie flat on the floor with your arms at approximately 45 degrees from your body. If this is uncomfortable for your lower back, roll up a blanket and place it under your knees.

Rest in this pose with no agenda. Be still and let go. This is not the time to nap, but to relax. Breathe normally and allow your mind to quiet. Observe your thoughts as they float by without getting involved in the conversation. Let go of judgments. Just be. The more you practice, the easier and more delightful this becomes.

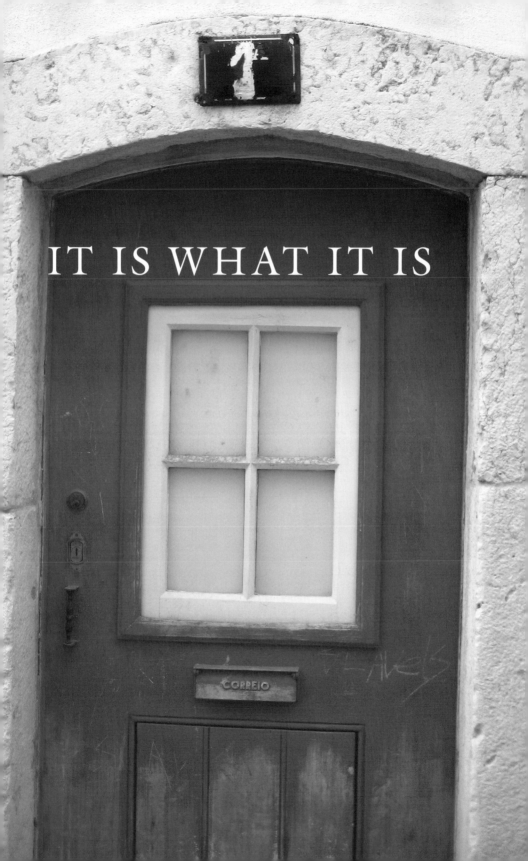

IT IS WHAT IT IS

My daughters are home from college now. For a little while, that is. Our home came alive the minute they arrived with their college possessions and endless loads of laundry. It is filled with a busy, lively, interactive energy. Our family feels complete.

I am spending a lot of time with Rachel, who is only home for a short time before she leaves for an international summer internship program. We share several common interests. Our relationship feels full and rich.

Full and rich. For the first time in a long time, I am keenly aware that my relationship with Kyle lacks that fullness. I feel sad about that. I'm not sure why I have become more aware of this now. It's not as if it hasn't been this way all along. Perhaps it's because my kids are all young adults now. Everything is changing.

I shared this with Kathy, my good friend, and coauthor of *It's All About Attitude*, during one of our bimonthly phone calls.

"It is what it is!" she blurted out.

Pause.

"Yes, it is," I said.

"That about says it all," we chimed in unison.

There was nothing else to say. I took a deep breath and relaxed. A weight seemed to drop off my shoulders. I felt lighter.

The girls are evolving in leaps and bounds. Kyle is evolving in tiny baby steps, sometimes visible only to his parents, and those few who know him very well. This is what is. He works with many obstacles just to make small connections with us. No, it's not the kind of relationship I have with my girls. They are oranges and he is an apple.

"It is what it is" lightens my load and frees me to live well with what is. It helps me stop making comparisons and appreciate Kyle for who he is, right now, and tomorrow, and for all the days that follow.

It is what it is.

Oxygen-Rich Tool

I invite you to make this your mantra. Whatever the "it" is, it is what it is.

Most things in life are out of our control. "It is what it is" has the power to transport us to that place of acceptance, even if just for a moment. Say it in your mind, or let it roll off your tongue. Take a few minutes and write it on some post-it notes, and place them strategically around your life areas. Let this phrase do its magic for you.

EXERCISE

Is there a magic potion for thriving, instead of merely surviving the challenging journey of life with a child who has autism? I've decided there is.

It's exercise.

The journey with a special child is a marathon, not a sprint. Regular exercise is an essential ingredient to staying in the race. Not only does it keep me on top of the game, it keeps me *in* the game. It's a key component to filling and refilling my mental, emotional, and spiritual well. It's my automatic attitude adjuster and energy booster.

I walk, I hike, I swim, I bike, I lift, and I do yoga. Some days, I think I don't have the time, or I'm not in the mood. If possible, I exercise anyway because those are the times I likely need it the most. Exercise produces endorphins, and endorphins make us happy. It is vital nourishment for my soul, and for loving and living well with autism and all of life's challenges.

Exercise is my magic potion in the autism marathon. It is the fuel that has enabled me to stay in the race for more than twenty-five years. It helps me take better care of Kyle and the rest of my family.

Oxygen-Rich Tool

Find a form of exercise you enjoy, or will tolerate, and do it. Thirty minutes is ideal, but even five minutes on a regular basis will have an effect. If you can't get out, run or walk up and down your stairs, do jumping jacks, do push ups, or dance wildly and vigorously around your living room. Consistency is ideal, but inconsistency is a great start.

BREATHE NOW,
FOR NOURISHMENT

Stop, just for this moment, and take a deep breath. Breathe deeply, filling your belly as well as your lungs. Count as you breathe in. Count as you breathe out. Breathe in and out for the same number of counts. Do this for as long as you can. Even just a minute can make a difference, as it did today.

I felt as if I had already put in a full day, yet I had only been awake for two hours. The morning had been packed full of challenges with Kyle. Some mornings are like that. We raced against the clock so he could be ready for his 7:30 a.m. pickup. Somehow, we managed to succeed. I dashed out the door to get to yoga class on time, leaving behind a trail of ruin in the kitchen.

My mind and body were still moving at 100 mph when I arrived at the studio, slipped off my shoes, and unrolled my yoga mat. I wasn't sure if I would be able to settle down mentally or physically. I had a lot on my plate for the remainder of the day and personal and business issues were floating around in my head. At that moment, yoga seemed like an indulgence.

We began with breathing. Breathe in for four, pause, breathe out for four, pause, repeat. It's impossible to count, notice my breath, and figure out my Thanksgiving menu all at the same time. After a while, my mind began to settle. The mental chatter faded into the background, and I felt myself become calm.

It always seems to come back to the breath. It's simple and requires no special equipment. It just requires a few moments of intention and attention. Taking the time to breathe with awareness can actually feel like a luxury. I find when I am resisting, or don't believe I have the time, is actually when I need it the most.

Breathing is the only autonomic function we have that also can be consciously controlled. It is nourishment for body and mind.

Oxygen-Rich Tool

It's quick. It's simple. It's free. Breathe in for four counts, pause, breathe out for four counts, pause, repeat. Blow your belly up with breath. Feel it rise through your diaphragm up to the tips of your lungs. Even one breath is enough to make a difference.

HEART'S DESIRE

I was jolted into action by the story of a man in Kyle's day program. About a year ago, he lost his parents and his sister in an accident. He now lives in a group home. There are days he just sits and cries. I do not know his exact level of comprehension. It doesn't matter. His loss is profound.

When I see this man, I imagine how lost and alone he feels. I am moved by his circumstances, and can't help but think of my own family. What would happen to Kyle in such a situation? I shudder and push the thoughts away, but they keep reappearing. Thus, the jolt.

Years ago, we updated our special needs trust and put all the financial details for Kyle's future in order, retaining a special attorney to ensure things were done properly. Good. This is done. What I have not done is set to paper other important details I desire for Kyle's future – my heart's desire.

What are my hopes and dreams for Kyle when we are no longer here to manage his life? Who are the best people to be his advocates? While I certainly can't control what happens, I can make the details of my wishes known. I can offer suggestions, and perhaps wisdom, so things are the best they can be for Kyle.

I am compelled to act. It feels overwhelming, but I am officially embarking on this project. In the end, I know it will be good to have it completed, tucked away, and sitting in my treasure chest. It's been something I've wanted to do for quite some time.

So, I sat down to write, to put on paper what is in my heart. Surely, if I can write books, I can create a plan for Kyle's future. So, why did the blank computer screen seem so daunting? The words did not come. That envelope of thought just was not opening. Perhaps too many emotions are involved.

After drawing a series of blanks, and then more blanks, I decided I would have to approach this in micro-movements, also known as baby steps. First, I removed myself from the computer and percolated on the question: what do I see for Kyle's future? I tossed the question up in the air, and over the next few days, allowed the insights to rain down upon me. I received no big revelations, only small tidbits. I scribbled them down when they came.

As of now, I am still listening for wisdom. I have yet to write a complete plan of action, but I do have a list of thoughts that will lead me to that plan. I aim to give it my best shot.

Oxygen-Rich Tool

Join me. Take this on in small bites if you need to. Think, feel, reflect, list – start to create an action plan by taking baby steps. This is an investment in the future of someone you love, as well as in your own peace of mind.

JUST ONE THING

Yesterday was a rough day for Kyle. Stress, anxiety, and behavior we usually don't see. He just wasn't himself. It was all there when I picked him up from his day program to go to music therapy. I knew it was going to be an interesting music session.

As I watched from the observation room, Kyle was having very little to do with making music. He pushed nearly everything away. He seemed to be fully engaged in what I call "Kyle-land" – that inner sanctum he goes to when he doesn't want to be bothered with anything.

Admittedly, I was feeling disappointed. I had driven a long way for what appeared to be no progress, or certainly not very much. When the session was over, I went into the music room for my usual chat with the therapists. Typically, we celebrate all the ways in which Kyle participated that day, small or large. Often, there are many. Some very amazing musical moments have taken place in that room.

"Today was all about Kyle," Kathleen commented. "But, he WAS able to do some cool things."

"You'll have to point it out to me," I said, with a hint of sarcasm, but a genuine desire to hear about the good for that day.

Kathleen shared that though he appeared to be elsewhere, he was singing (humming) in harmony when they were playing in his preferred keys. One of Kyle's gifts is his ability to harmonize. When they switched to unfamiliar keys, he made some unsuccessful attempts to find the key, but at the very end of the goodbye song – the very last beat of the entire session – he found it! In harmony, he belted out the final note.

Once again, Kyle defied appearances, as well as our beliefs. He had connected musically. He was there. It just took someone listening with a tuned ear to notice.

It's all about noticing that one thing. This is what makes my life rich. Joy and delight are found in the tiny details of my experiences – good feelings I get to take home with me. It only takes one. Just one thing.

Oxygen-Rich Tool

It's your turn to make life rich. Notice just one thing today. Is your child having a rough day? Are you? Find just one thing. Share it with someone or write it down. Blow it up and make it a highlight, a moment in your mind or on the page. Find just one thing.

MENTOR

Back and forth, back and forth, we slowly moved in unison as we held on to the broomstick (minus the brush). We sat across from each other with the broomstick horizontally between us at chest level. We both contributed the perfect amount of tension on the stick to maintain the flow.

Suddenly, we stopped. Mother and son gazed into each other's eyes for what felt like forever. We were momentarily suspended in time, connected by a stick. Together, we each used just enough energy to keep the broomstick suspended without moving at all. It was a special moment of stillness.

Through this process, I take on the role of mentor. On a physiological level, I help give Kyle a concrete example of the give and take, and the tension, that occur within all interactions. Just as in relationships, there are slight adjustments each partner must make to maintain the flow. We were indeed flowing.

The world often moves too quickly for Kyle. As a mentor, or guide, I slow things down and simplify them to help him process and participate in the blur we call life. As my apprentice, he has learned to trust me and allow me to guide him. The "mentor-apprentice" relationship is somewhat new for us. The relationship has evolved over the last few years, and it is one I have grown to enjoy. I believe Kyle takes pleasure in it, too.

Oxygen-Rich Tool

Take a moment to reflect and be grateful for mentors. Who have your mentors been, and what have they meant to you? Are you a mentor to someone in your life? If not, why not try it?

JEWELS

My children are my "jewels of delight." The author, Jill Badonsky, coined that phrase, and it perfectly expresses how I feel about them. They are precious gems, and I get to enjoy them.

When I started the car this morning, the CD player was playing "Angel." This happens to be one of my favorite songs. A few seconds into listening, I realized I was hearing my daughter! I turned up the volume and listened as her voice and guitar filled the car, and filled me. Better than any cup of coffee, I received a grande jolt of delight.

Rewind to last night. My husband, Neil, called me into the living room. He and Kyle were at the piano. Neil wanted to share an experience with Kyle, create a moment. We had no idea it would turn out to be, in my husband's words, "the coolest session we have ever had." Not only was Kyle taking turns at the piano, but more importantly, he was making the effort to turn and look at his dad, referencing him for his reaction. At one point, he even gestured to Neil to take his turn. I saw a softness about my son as he made a deep connection with his father. In fact, they both seemed to soften. I watched with delight as father and son became front-page news in my world that evening.

I spotlight these moments with my children. For me, being with them is all about slowing down and immersing myself in these moments – their moments. I feel proud, and even awe-inspired, by who they are, and what they continue to accomplish.

Oxygen-Rich Tool

Ready, set, notice. Find yourself a beautiful journal and go on a mission. Your mission is to notice and record the moments that bring you delight – your jewels of delight. In those moments when you need support, you will reconnect to your joy by rereading these jewels of delight.

SCARY

do
one
thing
every
day
that
scares
you
(eleanor roosevelt)

I see this quotation everyday. It is on a greeting card that sits on the counter in my bathroom. One of my friends, a former volunteer who worked with Kyle many years ago, gave it to me. She sent it to me to celebrate the release of my first book. On the inside of the card she wrote, "I think writing a book, publishing it, and putting your innermost thoughts out there counts as something scary."

My friend is right. It can be scary to put your innermost thoughts out there, but no more so than many other things we do, or could do.

Yesterday, I was hiking in the mountains and noticed how I walk the same routes all the time, even though there are many others I could take. A few of those routes scare me because of how narrow, steep, and slippery they are. I usually avoid those routes, but yesterday, I decided to shake things up a bit.

I took one of the scary routes. I put one foot in front of the other until I stood at the top, on the ledge, looking out over the Valley. What a feeling of exhilaration! I had made it! And, the journey up wasn't even as scary as I had remembered from previous hikes. Okay, I still had to get down, but so far, so good.

I did my "one thing." At that moment, I felt I could conquer anything. This one thing was enough to energize me for the entire day!

It can be scary to climb that steep, rugged mountain. It can be scary to take your autistic child out in public. However, there is something extremely empowering about feeling scared and doing it anyway.

Oxygen-Rich Tool

Do something today that scares you.

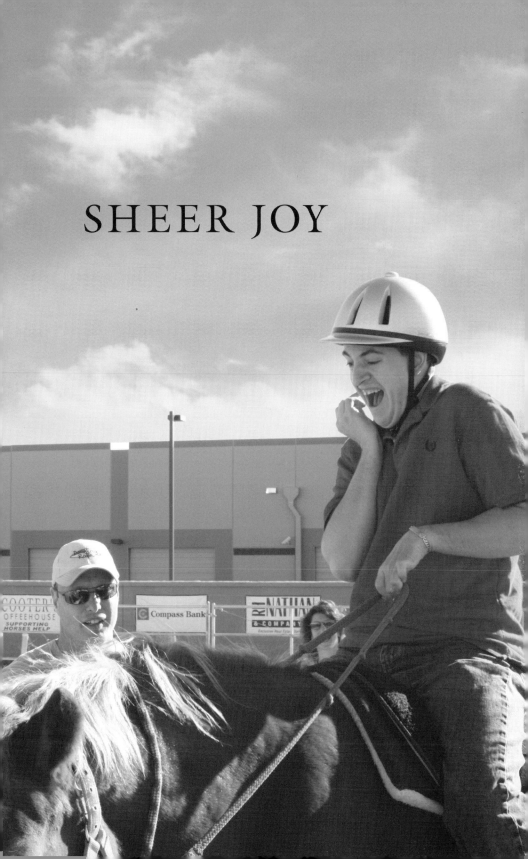

SHEER JOY

The sun had just gone down. There was a slight hint in the air that fall might be arriving shortly. With summer leaving, last night was Kyle's first time back on the horse after a three-month hiatus. The summer heat in Phoenix is just too brutal for riding.

I watched Kyle mount his horse flawlessly, and ride off with a big grin on his face. And to think, before he began twelve years ago, I didn't believe he would be able to ride. Good thing Dad thought otherwise.

Kyle rode his horse in sheer joy. With his side-walker, Clint, he walked, interspersed with moments of trotting. You could hear the rhythmic clip clop of the horse's feet, and Clint's encouragement. With chunks of silence as the backdrop, Kyle moved with the horse in a natural rocking motion. No distractions. Kyle's body settled way down. He was in his element.

I was in my element, too. After all these years, I still get a thrill when I watch. I'm so grateful we stumbled upon an activity Kyle can enjoy so much.

Technically, the type of horseback riding Kyle does is called hippo-therapy. People with special needs or medical conditions receive enormous therapeutic value from riding a horse.

Many have asked what Kyle gets from his biweekly rides – how it has helped him. My answer is always the same: he loves it. That's enough for me. His precious quality of life is enhanced because he experiences the sheer joy of riding a horse. It is one of his passions. It matters not whether he ever achieves a certain life skill or goal through horseback riding. What matters is the smile on his face, and that serene expression he gets when the horse comes to a stop and the ride is over.

Sheer joy. That's what he receives from riding. In those moments, that's all he needs. I also receive my dose of sheer joy just watching Kyle get his.

Oxygen-Rich Tool

Have you had a taste of sheer joy recently? It's delicious, even in tiny bites, What gives you sheer joy? Seek it out. Do it.

WISHES

I was asked to speak at an event, "Wishes for the Future," sponsored by a local nonprofit. This nonprofit supports parents of children with special needs. This was a time of upheaval and transition for Kyle and me, so I used it as an opportunity to ask and explore the answers to a very important question: What are my wishes for Kyle, my young adult son who is deeply affected by autism? Here they are:

- He needs something to do each day to make his life meaningful. His life CAN be meaningful.

- He needs to continue to make a difference in this world, or the community in which he lives, each day. He has already made a difference, and he CAN continue to do so.

- He needs a place where he can continue to learn and grow. We do not know how much he is capable of learning and achieving, and we must not let labels limit him. He demonstrates daily that he CAN learn and grow.

- He needs to be in a place where the expectations are high, and those around him look beyond what they see on the outside to nurture, support, and challenge his potential. He CAN rise to those expectations, but only if we dare to have them.

- He needs us to stand by him with unending patience, support and encouragement, never giving up. With awareness, we CAN be there for him in these ways.

- He needs to experience those feelings of accomplishment for completing something challenging or difficult. When we provide the experiences, he CAN achieve those "I did it!" moments. Moments all of us can be proud of.

- Most importantly, he needs connection. He needs the intimacy that occurs when two people are in a relationship and have a bond. We know what it looks and feels like, and it's also apparent when it's missing. This will take more effort on the part of those working with him because connection is not one of his strong points. They may have to work a bit harder to find a way, but it has been done before, and it CAN be done again.

The opportunities that exist after the high school years for young adults with special needs are extremely limited. They seem to drop off the radar. Adult day care is not going to grant my wishes. My wish for the future is something much, much better.

What are my wishes for Kyle and others with special needs? Quality of life. Happiness and joy. Accomplishment and meaning. Good times. Relationships. Independence. Employment. It's up to those of us who care to create these opportunities.

Oxygen-Rich Tool

What are your wishes for the future? Are you on the right road to realizing them, or do you need to make some course corrections? Gift yourself with the time to think about them, talk about them, and even write them down.

ZEN

The emergency room physician walked in and said, "Wow, I should just stay in HERE all evening. It's so calm and peaceful. Your son has a zen quality about him."

At that moment, he did. In the way he knew how, he was trying to quiet his racing pulse, calm his anxiety of the unknown, and possibly even block out the throbbing pain. Maybe, at that moment, his autism – his ability to go deep within – was his gift.

Kyle was in the emergency room waiting to have his hand x-rayed. He had been in a serious car accident and had broken his finger when the air bag deployed. He was one lucky young man, and we were one grateful set of parents. His injuries easily could have been much worse.

He was sitting very calmly. As he sat, he hummed a low, soft, vibratory sound – ahhhh, ahhhh, ahhhh. The tone and tune were constant. Kyle went within himself to find a quiet spot from which to cope. The doctor was right. He was most definitely zen.

Through toning, he was breathing rhythmically. I, too, have found breathing rhythmically to be a great way to slow down, calm down, or pull myself back into the present moment when my mind is racing.

There is something especially calming about "noisy breathing" – creating a vibration in the back of the throat. My mind attaches itself to that sound. I've found it is almost impossible to pay attention to that sound and have a busy mind at the same time. The effect for me is similar to Kyle's toning. Peace. Zen.

Oxygen-Rich Tool

Try this. Make time for ten focused breaths. You have to breathe anyway, right? Practice what the yogis call ujjayi breath, or loud breathing.

Here's how you do it: Take a deep, inhaling breath, and then constrict your throat as you exhale. You exhale with the glottis held partially closed. You should hear a throaty sound when you exhale. It has the same sound as the one you make when you are fogging up a mirror by breathing on it. It's a long "ha" sound.

When you've got this, try it with your lips closed. You can create a noisy sound on the inhaling breath as well. Focus on making the breath slow and steady. This is an awesome tool when the going gets tough, or simply to remind yourself to pause within the busyness of your day and refocus your energy and attention.

EPILOGUE: READY TO LAUNCH

Throughout this book, I have endeavored to provide you with oxygen-rich tools to help you love and live well with your child. I hope you have found them valuable and useful.

Yet, as I write this final chapter, I realize I have left one very big challenge unaddressed – launching our children from the nest. When will they be ready? When will we? Where will they go?

These are tough questions. I wonder when Kyle will be ready to launch. More accurately, I wonder when I will be ready to launch Kyle.

With my daughter, Rachel, there is no question. She is ready to launch. With college graduation just behind her, she is beginning her adult life. She has worked hard to get to this point, and I am excited for her. Even in these uncertain economic times, her future is bright with opportunity. I don't worry about her. I have full confidence that she is prepared to face the world and will thrive wherever she ends up.

With Kyle, I am frequently asked whether he will be able to live independently. Kyle does not have the skills or the judgment to take care of himself, so the answer is no. I do not have the same confidence in Kyle's future as I do in Rachel's.

This is a scary place for me, and one I have not delved into very deeply. I am not yet ready to launch Kyle, but am keenly aware that the day will come when, ready or not, I must face the decision. Where will he live, and who will take care of him? These are the questions that remain tucked away for future consideration.

So, I just keep putting one foot in front of the other. I hope for the best, trusting the answer lies in the future. With so many children being diagnosed these days, there will eventually be a flood of adults who need supported-living situations – new opportunities that have yet to come into existence.

For now, Kyle waits on the launch pad, and I stand firmly beside him. I release the need to know right now. When the time comes, I trust I will be able to let go and allow Kyle to move forward with grace and ease. In the meantime, I hope, pray, and trust.

Oxygen-Rich Tool

Here is what I have to offer you: hope, pray, and trust. Believe that the best will happen for your child. Let go. Love. Most importantly, breathe.

About the Author

Gayle has a lifelong connection to autism through her brother, Philip, and her son, Kyle. She holds a BA in special education, is an inspirational speaker and parent mentor, and is the coauthor of *It's All About Attitude: Loving and Living Well with Autism*. Gayle directed an intensive home therapy program for eleven years for her son, Kyle. During that time, she trained more than one hundred therapists and aides. Gayle resides in Phoenix, Arizona with her family.

Clockwise from left: Leah, Neil, Rachel, Kyle and Gayle Nobel